Alex Takedzo

Is My Boss Stupid?

Understanding Misjudged Leadership: From Frustration to Professional Growth

© Alex Takedzo, 2024

Navigating the complexities of workplace dynamics, particularly with demanding supervisors, is a challenge every professional encounters. Mastering Boss Management provides a practical guide to not only surviving but thriving in high-pressure environments. This insightful book explores the art of managing relationships with challenging bosses, fostering collaboration, and transforming professional hurdles into opportunities for growth.

Content

Introduction: The Art of Managing Complex Work Relationships........................4
    Relevance of the Issue in Modern Society..5
    Key Issues:..5
    Differences in Values and Priorities:..5
    Incompetence and Micromanagement:.. 5
    Emotional Burnout:..6
    Psychological Approach: Why Bosses Can Seem "Difficult"............................6
    Purpose of the Book: Thriving Despite Difficulties..6
    Conflict Management and Active Listening:.. 6
    Emotional Resilience and Self-Reflection:.. 6
    Negotiation Psychology:... 6
    Work-Life Balance:...7
    Turning Challenges into Growth Opportunities:... 7
Book Summary.. 7
    Chapter 1: Understanding the Perceived "Foolish" Boss................................. 7
    Chapter 2: Empathy and Perspective Taking..8
    Chapter 3: Effective Communication Strategies... 8
    Chapter 4: Building Trust and Understanding... 8
    Chapter 5: Leveraging Opportunities in Difficult Situations.............................8
    Chapter 6: Self-Care and Well-Being.. 9
    Chapter 7: Overcoming Obstacles and Challenges..9
    Chapter 8: Turning Conflict into Collaboration... 9
Chapter 1: Understanding the Perceived "Foolish" Boss..11
    Reasons for Perceiving a Boss as Incompetent.. 11
    Overcoming Personal Biases and Cognitive Distortions................................. 15
    Methods for Evaluating Your Boss...22
    Conclusion: Objective Perception as a Key to Better Relationships.............. 25
Chapter 2: Empathy and Perspective-Taking..25
    Developing Empathy for Your Boss's Position... 27
    Practicing Changing Perspective..27
    The Method of "Realistic Empathy"..28
    Evaluating and Gathering Feedback from Colleagues....................................29
    Constructive Perception of Difficult Decisions.. 30
    Overcoming Differences in Communication Styles... 31
    Tips for Problem-Solving and Reducing Tension...32
    Conclusion...32
Chapter 3: Effective Communication Strategies..32
    Clear and Concise Communication...33
    Avoiding Conflicts Through Clear Communication...34
    Navigating Communication Challenges..39
    Developing Empathy...40
    Constructive Communication for Conflict Resolution.................................... 41

    Evaluating Your Manager's Communication Style.. 42
    Conclusion.. 43
Chapter 4: Building Trust and Understanding.. 44
    Methods for Building Trust... 45
    Mutual Respect as a Key Element.. 46
    Examples and Tips for Problem-Solving..47
    Conclusion.. 50
Chapter 5: Finding Opportunities in Difficult Situations......................................51
    Strategies for Leveraging Challenges...52
    Scientific Foundation.. 53
    Learning from Mistakes... 55
    Problem-Solving Tips..56
    Conclusion..57
Chapter 6: Self-Care and Well-Being.. 58
    Managing Stress and Emotional Burnout...58
    Maintaining Work-Life Balance...59
    Tips for Problem-Solving.. 61
    Conclusion.. 61
Chapter 7: Overcoming Obstacles and Challenges..62
    Building Resilience.. 62
    Shifting Perception.. 63
    Practical Steps for Reframing Challenges..65
    Developing "Soft Power"... 65
    Developing a Problem-Solving Strategy.. 67
    SWOT Analysis in Problem-Solving... 69
Chapter 8: Turning Conflict into Collaboration.. 71
    Understanding the Nature of Conflict.. 72
    Using Negotiation Techniques... 72
    Building a Common Goal... 75
    Tips for Problem-Solving.. 77
Conclusion: The Art of Harmony in the Workplace..79
    Adaptability as a Key Skill...79
    Self-Management as the Ultimate Mastery... 80
    Viewing Difficult Experiences as Opportunities for Growth............. 82
    Harmonious Workplace Relationships: A Path to Professional Mastery.......... 83

Introduction: The Art of Managing Complex Work Relationships

Working in a corporate environment involves constant interaction with diverse personalities, each contributing unique traits, values, and behaviors to the workplace. Among the many factors that influence career success, the quality of relationships with management holds a special place. Often, employees find themselves dealing with a boss who seems incompetent, inconsistent, or even outright "foolish." How do we handle these situations?

This book focuses on developing skills to build productive working relationships, even with managers whose decisions may appear illogical and ineffective. Often, the problem lies not only in the boss's actions, but also in how we perceive their behavior. Successful interaction requires patience, emotional resilience, and communication management. Understanding workplace relationship psychology opens up opportunities for both personal and professional growth, regardless of the difficulty of the circumstances.

Relevance of the Issue in Modern Society

The challenge of difficult relationships with management is relevant for most employees today. According to surveys, up to 75% of workers report that strained relationships with their boss are a major cause of workplace stress and burnout. Communication difficulties and a lack of trust can lead to low motivation, decreased productivity, and high employee turnover. In an era where many companies are adopting hybrid or remote work models, managing such conflicts becomes even more complicated due to limited face-to-face interaction.

Key Issues:

Lack of Clear Communication: Managers may fail to clearly convey their expectations or change priorities at the last minute, leaving employees feeling uncertain.

Differences in Values and Priorities:

Conflicts often arise from mismatched goals and approaches between a manager and their team. For instance, a boss might prioritize quick results, while employees focus on quality.

Incompetence and Micromanagement:

Employees typically perceive excessive control or a lack of leadership skills as signs of incompetence, leading to frustration and irritation.

Emotional Burnout:

Poorly thought-out actions by managers can contribute to burnout, especially if employees feel unsupported or unappreciated.

Psychological Approach: Why Bosses Can Seem "Difficult"

Perceiving a manager as incompetent is influenced not only by their actual behavior but also by the cognitive and emotional biases of employees. People tend to seek confirmation of their expectations—if someone is initially perceived as incompetent, any action they take will be viewed through that lens. Psychological studies show that our reactions to others' behavior are often determined by our own mental attitudes and stress.

Moreover, managers are under pressure too: they must deliver results, handle limited resources, and balance the expectations of subordinates and higher-ups. Understanding this can help shift the focus from blame to problem-solving.

Purpose of the Book: Thriving Despite Difficulties

This book offers tools and techniques to develop skills for effective interaction with managers in challenging situations. Instead of resisting or avoiding engagement, you will learn to turn difficult situations into opportunities for growth and professional development.

We will explore the following key areas:

Conflict Management and Active Listening:

How to find common ground with your boss and reduce tension.

Emotional Resilience and Self-Reflection:

How to cope with disappointments and turn them into motivation for growth.

Negotiation Psychology:

How to build trust and achieve compromises.

Work-Life Balance:

How to care for your well-being, even when work is stressful.

Turning Challenges into Growth Opportunities:

It is important to remember that a successful career is built not only on achieving results, but also on handling difficulties.

Every challenge you face at work is an opportunity for self-improvement. Working with "difficult" managers teaches valuable skills: patience, diplomacy, emotional control, and the ability to find compromises. These qualities are valuable not only in professional life but also in personal relationships.

Ultimately, your ability to manage relationships with your boss is not just about surviving in a challenging corporate environment but a key to thriving. The more you invest in developing your communication and emotional resilience skills, the more successful and confident you will feel in any workplace.

Book Summary

Chapter 1: Understanding the Perceived "Foolish" Boss

Reasons for Perceiving a Boss as Incompetent:

- Illusion of Competence and High Expectations: Sometimes, our assessment of someone's abilities is biased. We tend to expect more from our bosses than they may realistically deliver.
- Differences in Priorities: What matters to an employee may not align with the boss's priorities. These differences are often misinterpreted as "incompetence."
- Personal Management Style: If a boss's leadership style doesn't match our expectations, we may view it as a weakness or lack of skill.

Overcoming Personal Biases:

- Cognitive Reframing Method: Learn to rethink your perception of the situation by objectively evaluating your boss's actions.
- Self-Understanding: Personal ambitions or perfectionism can amplify feelings of disappointment in your boss.

Chapter 2: Empathy and Perspective Taking

Developing Empathy for Your Boss's Position:

- Recognize that your boss may have limitations and face pressure from above. They, too, are part of a complex system.

Practicing Perspective Shifts:

- Use the "realistic empathy" method: try to understand the reasoning behind your boss's decisions. Even if they seem foolish, there are reasons worth considering.

Chapter 3: Effective Communication Strategies

Clear and Concise Communication:

- Be specific and straightforward. Use the "SBAR" method (Situation, Background, Assessment, Recommendation) to convey information.
- Present alternative solutions rather than merely pointing out problems.

Avoiding Conflicts through Clear Communication:

- Clarify and confirm to prevent misunderstandings. Use active listening to show genuine interest.

Chapter 4: Building Trust and Understanding

Methods for Building Trust:

- Perform your work at a high level: professionalism builds trust.
- Avoid gossip and demonstrate loyalty, even in difficult times.

Mutual Respect as a Key Element:

- Respect your boss's time and decisions, even if you disagree. Find ways to disagree constructively.

Chapter 5: Leveraging Opportunities in Difficult Situations

Finding Hidden Opportunities:

- Working with a difficult boss can sometimes open the door to developing new skills, like flexibility, creativity, and stress resilience.

Learning from Mistakes:

- Document situations where problems arose and analyze how you could have handled them differently. This increases your competence.

Chapter 6: Self-Care and Well-Being

Managing Stress and Emotional Burnout:

- Use relaxation techniques like breathing exercises and meditation.
- Stick to a rest schedule and make time for hobbies and social connections.

Maintaining Work-Life Balance:

- Remember: successful work relationships are impossible without taking care of your own well-being.

Chapter 7: Overcoming Obstacles and Challenges

Building Resilience:

- Learn to see difficult situations as opportunities for growth. Develop "soft power"—the ability to find solutions under challenging conditions.

Creating a Problem-Solving Strategy:

- Develop an action plan for difficult scenarios, like handling criticism or unpredictable decisions from your boss.

Chapter 8: Turning Conflict into Collaboration

Using Negotiation Techniques:

- Listen more than you speak and find common ground. Use phrases like, "How do you see this situation?"

Building a Shared Goal:

- Foster collaboration around the company's common goals. When everyone works toward the same outcome, differences become less significant.

In the dynamic atmosphere of today's work environment, the relationships between employees and their bosses often resemble a complex maze. Every interaction with a manager—whether positive or negative—not only shapes a person's career path but also affects their sense of satisfaction and success. But what happens when a boss is perceived as incompetent? How do you manage a situation where the manager is thought of as "foolish"?

This book, "Is My Boss Stupid? Understanding Misjudged Leadership: From Frustration to Professional Growth", offers a deep analysis of such situations and practical strategies for those who face these challenges. Throughout the pages, we will break down the complexities of workplace relationships and illuminate how interactions with such managers can become a launchpad for growth and development.

In each chapter, we explore key principles for effectively managing your boss. We start by examining the reasons why a boss might be perceived as "foolish" and discuss how our own biases influence this perception.

Next, we delve into developing empathy and the ability to see things from your boss's perspective. This becomes a crucial tool for successfully navigating difficult workplace relationships.

Communication is the foundation of any relationship, including professional ones. In the third chapter, we discuss effective communication strategies and offer practical tips for clear and precise expression. Developing these skills will help reduce misunderstandings and conflicts.

Trust and understanding are equally important aspects. In the fourth chapter, we explore methods for building trust-based relationships that foster productive collaboration built on mutual respect.

Where some see only difficulties, others find opportunities. The fifth chapter teaches us to rethink challenging situations and uncover hidden opportunities for growth.

The sixth chapter reminds us of the importance of self-care. In a high-pressure professional environment, maintaining a work-life balance is crucial for emotional well-being.

The seventh chapter focuses on overcoming obstacles. Developing resilience and problem-solving skills will not only help you handle difficulties but also emerge stronger from them.

Finally, in the eighth chapter, we discuss transforming conflicts into opportunities for collaboration. Using negotiation techniques, we will learn to find shared goals and build harmonious interactions with our bosses.

Throughout the book, recurring concepts, methods, exercises, and examples are intentionally repeated. While some may find this repetitive, it emphasizes the importance of these elements for achieving success. The author deliberately returns to key points to reinforce them in practice, helping readers gain a deeper understanding and assimilation of the ideas. This approach serves as a reminder that mastery requires consistent repetition and implementation of core principles, and it should be taken as a sign to pay particular attention to these aspects.

In the end, this book is not just a guide, but a roadmap for personal and professional growth. Join this journey to turn challenges into opportunities and learn to thrive even in the most difficult work environments.

Chapter 1: Understanding the Perceived "Foolish" Boss

In the broad palette of professional life, few relationships are as crucial—or as tense—as those between an employee and their boss.

For many, the mere mention of the word "boss" evokes a complex range of emotions, from admiration and respect to disappointment and frustration. But what happens when this figure of authority is perceived as incompetent? How do we navigate the intricacies of workplace dynamics when our boss is, perhaps unfairly, labeled "foolish"?

Before we start solving this puzzle, it is essential to first understand the underlying reasons why a boss may be perceived this way. In this chapter, we will embark on a journey of self-analysis and exploration, examining the multifaceted factors that contribute to the perception of a "foolish" boss.

Seeing a boss as incompetent or "foolish" is not uncommon in a work environment. However, such an opinion is often shaped by cognitive and emotional factors, as well as differences in priorities and expectations. This chapter will break down why employees might feel their boss isn't handling responsibilities well and how to avoid perception errors by using self-analysis and objective evaluation techniques.

Reasons for Perceiving a Boss as Incompetent

1. Illusion of Competence and High Expectations

We often place exaggerated expectations on our bosses, believing that a leader should be competent in every area and make only the best decisions. When reality falls short of these expectations, cognitive dissonance arises, and the boss appears "foolish." This perception is also linked to the illusion of control: employees may feel that the boss should foresee problems and prevent mistakes, even though perfect solutions rarely exist. This perception is a product of our exaggerated expectations and the illusion that a leader must manage everything flawlessly.

Example: An employee may criticize their boss for lacking technical expertise, forgetting that the primary role of the boss is to coordinate the team, not to be an expert in niche areas. Assessing a boss's competence should consider their actual role and priorities.

The Psychology of High Expectations and Illusion of Control.

The illusion of control is a cognitive bias where people overestimate their or others' ability to influence outcomes. Employees may expect their boss to foresee all risks and prevent mistakes. In reality, no leader has complete information or ideal solutions, especially in a rapidly changing world with limited resources.

Employees also tend to overemphasize a lack of expertise in specific areas, forgetting that the boss's main job is not to be a detail-oriented expert, but to coordinate the team and manage processes strategically.

Example: In a tech company, a manager might be criticized for not knowing the intricacies of programming, even though their main role is to coordinate teams and set priorities. Expecting the boss to be an expert in all aspects is unfair and hinders fair evaluation based on their true responsibilities.

Re-Evaluating Competence and the Real Priorities of a Boss.

It's important to remember that the key tasks of a manager are to oversee processes, allocate resources, and achieve team goals—not to solve specialized technical problems. For instance, an effective manager knows how to delegate tasks to those with the right expertise and focuses on maintaining productivity and employee motivation.

Tips for Changing Perception:

- Reassess Your Expectations: Recognize that leadership is not about knowing everything, but about effectively managing and guiding a team.

- Identify Your Boss's Strengths: Instead of focusing on their weaknesses, pay attention to the skills they excel at, whether it's organizing work, maintaining team spirit, or resolving conflicts.
- Shared Responsibility: Understand that team success is a joint effort, and employees play a crucial role in identifying and solving problems. Building a partnership with your boss, rather than opposing them, can improve collaboration.

Brief Conclusion:

The illusion of competence creates unnecessary tension and obstructs constructive workplace interactions. Realizing that a boss is not required to know everything or avoid all mistakes can reduce stress and foster productive relationships. Ultimately, the key to success is mutual understanding and collaboration, rather than fault-finding.

2. Differences in Priorities: The Issue of Perception and Value Conflicts.

Managers and employees often face differences in priorities, creating tension and dissatisfaction. This situation arises because managers are responsible for achieving strategic goals and meeting deadlines, while employees engaged in more operational roles focus on quality work and optimized processes. When these discrepancies are ignored, there is a risk that both sides will start to see each other as ineffective or uninterested in shared success.

The Importance of Understanding Different Priorities.

Managers typically concentrate on strategic vision, short-term KPIs, and cost minimization. For example, it may be crucial for a business to launch a product by a specific date, even if it means cutting some stages, like thorough testing. On the other hand, employees care about the process—striving for high-precision and flawless quality. These priority differences often appear as indifference to quality from one side or excessive perfectionism from the other.

Example: Conflict in Product Development Priorities

Imagine a scenario where a manager demands a reduction in testing time for new software to meet a set release date. Developers, understanding the risks, insist on more time to identify and fix bugs. From their perspective, cutting testing seems like irresponsible management, while from the manager's viewpoint, it is a necessary business compromise to maintain a competitive edge.

The Psychological Aspect of Priority Conflicts.

When employees don't understand the manager's motivations, they may feel that their work is undervalued and that only external metrics matter. On the flip side, managers might perceive employees as inflexible or unable to see the "big picture." This creates mutual distrust and a sense of incompetence on both sides.

How to Avoid Priority Conflicts?

- Open Discussion of Goals and Constraints: Discussing priorities early on helps both sides understand each other's motivations and limitations. For example, developers can explain the risks of insufficient testing, while the manager can justify the importance of deadlines.
- Finding Compromise Solutions: It may be possible to split the release into multiple phases or launch a version with basic functionality, refining it later. This approach balances both sides' priorities.
- Empathy and Acknowledgment of Differences: It's crucial to understand that both parties are invested in success, but their perspectives differ. Managers should respect employees' dedication to quality, while employees should accept the need for strategic decisions.

Tip:

Try to discuss priorities openly and in advance. Instead of viewing differences as a conflict, use them as an opportunity to develop flexible solutions that achieve strategic goals while maintaining high quality. Regular meetings and transparent communication can reduce misunderstandings and build stronger trust.

Brief Conclusion:

Priority differences are inevitable, but they don't have to lead to conflict. Recognizing that each side has its own tasks and focus is the first step toward constructive collaboration. Balancing business needs with team requirements not only reduces tension but also increases organizational efficiency.

3. Personal Management Style: How a Leader's Individuality Influences Perception

A leader's personality traits and management style significantly influence how their team perceives them. Depending on their temperament, experience, and beliefs, different managers use varied management styles—ranging from democratic to authoritarian. However, a style that one employee interprets as flexibility and trust may be seen by another as indifference or lack of control. Such disagreements often lead to misunderstandings and reduced trust.

Typical Management Styles and How They Are Perceived.

1. Delegating Style (Minimal Control):

Leaders who prefer to delegate tasks may believe in the importance of team autonomy and independence. However, some employees perceive this approach as a lack of leadership and feel they are not given adequate attention.

Example: A charismatic leader might inspire the team to achieve high goals but neglect operational details, leaving employees who need more structured support feeling dissatisfied.

Tip: If your manager gives you too much freedom, clarify their goals and expected outcomes. This will help strike a balance between independence and clear expectations.

2. Micromanagement (Strict Control)

Managers prone to micromanagement often believe that by closely overseeing tasks, they are ensuring quality and meeting deadlines. Yet, employees may perceive this as a lack of trust and find the constant oversight demotivating and confidence-draining.

Example: A boss might insist on reviewing every detail of a report before it is sent, slowing down work and causing frustration for employees accustomed to more independence.

Tip: In such situations, it's important to discuss boundaries of responsibility. Make sure your manager knows your level of competence and suggest a regular reporting format to reduce their need for excessive control.

The Psychological Factor: Why Leaders Choose Different Styles.

The choice of management style often depends on personal experience and beliefs. Leaders who have grown up in a strict corporate culture may see micromanagement as normal. In contrast, those trained in modern methods may lean toward granting the team more autonomy and fostering self-organization.

Cultural factors also play a significant role: some organizations value flexibility and informality, while others uphold strict adherence to hierarchy. Different management styles can lead to conflicts if employee expectations and a boss's habits do not align.

How to Adapt to Your Manager's Personal Style?

- Understanding Your Boss's Motives: Talk to your manager to understand why they manage the way they do. For instance, if they tend to micromanage, find out what specific concerns they have. This will help improve your working relationship.
- Flexibility in Communication: Adjust to your manager's style and tailor your communication accordingly. For example, with a delegating leader, initiate meetings to discuss ongoing tasks and maintain a strong connection.
- Building Trust: If your boss tends to be overly controlling, demonstrate your reliability and competence to reduce the need for constant oversight.

Brief Conclusion:

Different management styles can inspire or frustrate, depending on employee expectations. To work successfully with any manager, it's essential to develop empathy and flexibility. Try to understand your boss's motives and constraints and adapt to their style to avoid misunderstandings and conflicts. These skills will not only make your interactions smoother but also help you become a more effective leader in the future.

Overcoming Personal Biases and Cognitive Distortions.

1. Cognitive Reframing Method: Letting Go of Thought Stereotypes.

Cognitive reframing is a technique that allows you to view a challenging situation from a new, more constructive perspective. It helps you avoid getting stuck in negative emotions and stereotypes, and instead, find alternative explanations for others' actions or decisions. This method is commonly used in Cognitive Behavioral Therapy (CBT) to change automatic negative thoughts and in conflict management practices.

Why Does Cognitive Reframing Work?

When faced with actions or decisions that seem illogical or mistaken, people often experience irritation and stress. Reframing allows you to replace an emotional reaction with rational analysis. In a professional environment, this approach can:

- Reduce Bias: Help you avoid assuming that your boss's behavior is solely due to incompetence or unwillingness to help.
- Maintain Objectivity: Enable you to assess the situation, considering the constraints and priorities of others.
- Develop Empathy: Allow you to understand that even if your boss's decisions don't meet your expectations, they may be justified from their perspective.

Example of Using Cognitive Reframing:

If a manager cancels a project, employees may see it as a sign of irresponsibility or incompetence. Reframing prompts you to ask:

- Could it be that management learned of budget constraints and decided to reallocate resources?
- Might the project no longer align with the company's strategic goals?
- Perhaps external market changes required an urgent shift in focus?

Practical Exercise: Changing Your Perspective.

The next time your boss's actions cause frustration or confusion, try this exercise:

- Describe the situation and your initial reaction to it.
- List three possible explanations for why the decision might make sense from your boss's point of view.

- Reflect on how your emotional reaction changed after completing the exercise.

Example:
Situation: The manager suddenly changes priorities and assigns a new task.
Initial Reaction: Frustration over the disruption of your plan.
Possible Explanations:

- An urgent client request came in that cannot be ignored.
- The company faced external market changes requiring rapid adaptation.
- The manager received directives from higher up that had to be implemented without discussion.

Tip for Deeper Application:
Discuss your manager's decisions directly when appropriate. If their actions seem inconsistent, ask open-ended questions such as: "Can we understand what external factors influenced this?" or "What are the main priorities so we can better adjust our plan?" Open dialogue often relieves tension and leads to compromise solutions.

Brief Conclusion:
Cognitive reframing is a powerful tool for reducing stress and improving professional relationships. It not only helps you view the world in a more positive light but also builds adaptability and empathy. Over time, this technique makes interactions with management more productive, based on mutual understanding rather than criticism and dissatisfaction.

2. Understanding Your Biases and Ambitions: The Key to Reducing Tension.

Relationships with a boss are often complicated by personal ambitions, internal beliefs, and a tendency toward perfectionism. Employees striving for high achievements and rapid career advancement may feel disappointed if their manager prioritizes more pragmatic or gradual goals. Acknowledging your expectations and how they influence your perception of your boss helps prevent unnecessary conflicts and improve cooperation.

Ambitions as a Source of Stress.

Employees often discover that their career aspirations do not align with their boss's priorities. The desire for rapid advancement can clash with a manager's realistic strategy focused on steady progress and avoiding burnout. Ambitions, especially when coupled with perfectionism, can make an employee constantly dissatisfied with any compromise, interpreting it as incompetence.

Example: Consider an employee who aims to get promoted within six months or be involved in major projects. The manager, however, focuses on gradual development, offering assignments with less responsibility to prevent burnout. The employee might interpret this as a lack of confidence in their abilities or see the manager as unambitious, though it may actually reflect the manager's concern for long-term effectiveness.

Biases and Cognitive Distortions

Our expectations of what an "ideal" boss should be, are often a source of frustration. Subconsciously, we may hope that a manager will fully align with our goals and working methods. However, in reality, every leader operates based on their own priorities, experience, and limitations. Recognizing your biases can help you manage these contradictions and reduce stress.

Tip: Ask yourself, "Why does this decision trigger negative emotions in me? Is it related to my personal expectations and beliefs?" This simple step fosters self-reflection and helps identify the source of conflict.

The Boss's Perspective: Pragmatism vs. Perfectionism

Managers often make compromise decisions, considering resources, deadlines, and the company's overall strategy.

This approach may seem less than ideal to an employee, but it doesn't necessarily mean the manager is wrong. A pragmatic management style aims to distribute efforts efficiently and minimize risks.

Example: A boss may choose to complete a project with an acceptable level of quality to meet a deadline and free up resources for other tasks. A perfectionist employee may feel frustrated that the work wasn't done to the "ideal" standard, interpreting this as a lack of competence on the manager's part.

Practical Exercise for Self-Reflection

Try this exercise to better understand how your ambitions influence your interactions with your boss:

- Write down your main career goals and expectations for your current role.
- Assess how well your expectations align with the company's and your boss's priorities.
- Identify where your ambitions might hinder constructive dialogue and consider how to adjust them for better collaboration.

Brief Conclusion:

Understanding your ambitions and biases is an important step toward harmonious relationships with your boss. Not all leaders are obligated to match employees' ideals, and a pragmatic approach to management is often more effective in the long run. Developing self-reflection and embracing different management styles can reduce stress, improve professional relationships, and allow you to focus on productive work.

3. Seeking Feedback and Colleagues' Opinions: Expanding Your Perspective

Our perception of a boss is often limited to our own experiences and fragmented observations. To form a more objective opinion, it can be helpful to seek feedback from colleagues. Others may have different insights into the situation, potentially recognizing strengths and strategic motives in your boss's actions that you may have overlooked.

The Impact of Limited Information on Perception.

We often evaluate a manager based on our own expectations and emotions. This narrow view can lead to biased judgments, especially if the manager makes a decision that conflicts with our personal interests. In such cases, discussing the situation with colleagues can reveal new aspects of the boss's behavior and help adjust our perception.

Example: You might feel that your boss is avoiding responsibility when delegating tasks. However, colleagues could point out that this actually demonstrates trust in the team and fosters independence.

Benefits of Sharing Perspectives with the Team.

- Gain Different Viewpoints: Hearing how other team members view the boss's actions may provide new insights.
- Minimize Personal Biases: Colleagues can highlight facts you may have missed.
- Learn Adaptation Strategies: Team members who have already found effective ways to work with the boss can share helpful advice and tactics.

How to Request Feedback Properly?

- Frame Your Questions Neutrally: Avoid judgmental statements or complaints. Ask how colleagues perceive the boss's decisions and management style.
- Be Open to Criticism: If you hear opinions that differ from yours, try to approach them objectively, even if they challenge your viewpoint.
- Look for Common Themes: Identify patterns in the responses. If multiple colleagues mention the same traits of the boss, this can be valuable information for refining your perception.

Practical Exercise:

- Choose one or two trusted colleagues and ask them open-ended questions: "How do you perceive our boss? What are their strengths?"
- Record and analyze their answers: Do their opinions align with yours? What positive aspects might you have missed?
- Determine how you can use this information to improve your interaction with the boss.

Brief Conclusion:

Seeking colleagues' opinions is an effective way to eliminate perceptual distortions and see your boss's actions from a new angle. Instead of being trapped by your frustrations, openly explore how others view the same situation. This can help you better understand your boss and develop more productive strategies for collaboration.

4. Unconscious Biases and Stereotypes: How They Impact Perceptions of Leaders

Our evaluation of a boss is not always objective and may be influenced by deeply ingrained stereotypes. The image of an incompetent or indifferent manager is often shaped by societal and media-driven beliefs. These stereotypes create expectations that subsequently affect how we perceive real leaders.

How Stereotypes Distort Perception?

Stereotypes can influence workplace relationships, fostering mistrust or setting unrealistic expectations that do not align with reality. For instance, employees may believe that a successful leader should be of a certain age, gender, or have expertise in every area they manage.

Example: A young manager may face distrust from employees who expect a leader to have extensive experience. Even if the manager demonstrates high competence, perceptions of their effectiveness may still be affected by bias.

Common Stereotypes About Leaders:

- Age and Experience: Older managers are often viewed as more competent, while younger ones are seen as inexperienced and prone to mistakes.
- Gender Biases: Female leaders may face distrust, especially in traditionally "male-dominated" industries. Men, on the other hand, may be perceived as less empathetic and supportive.
- Leadership Stereotypes: A manager who avoids a directive style may be seen as weak, even if their approach is more effective in the long term.

How to Recognize and Overcome Biases

- Self-Reflection: Acknowledge that everyone has biases. Regularly analyze your thoughts and beliefs about your boss: which are based on experience, and which are rooted in bias?
- Evaluate Based on Results: Focus on assessing your boss's actual achievements and decisions, rather than how they conform to your expectations or stereotypes.
- Ask Open Questions: Instead of making assumptions, ask yourself: "Why do I think this? What is the basis of my perception?"

Practical Exercise:

- Write down three common stereotypes about leaders that may affect your perception.
- Reflect on how these biases might have distorted your assessment of your boss's actions.
- Over the next week, note instances where you notice these stereotypes influencing your judgment and replace them with objective criteria.

Brief Conclusion:

Awareness of your biases is a crucial step toward objectivity. When you evaluate your boss based on real achievements and qualities, rather than stereotypes, it not only improves workplace relationships but also helps you become a more mature and fair professional.

5. Communication Gaps: How They Impact Perceptions of a Manager.

Insufficient or ineffective communication often leads to negative perceptions of leadership. A manager may be highly competent, but if they cannot clearly convey their expectations or fail to listen to employees, they may seem incompetent or indifferent. Communication gaps erode trust, slow down task completion, and increase mistakes, which in turn lowers employee motivation.

How Communication Gaps Manifest in Practice?

- Vague Instructions: The manager provides unclear or ambiguous tasks, leaving employees unsure of what is expected.
- Lack of Feedback: Employees may feel that their work goes unnoticed if the manager does not provide timely or constructive feedback.
- Ignoring Employee Opinions: Leaders who don't ask for or ignore team input may be seen as indifferent or short-sighted.

Example: A manager assigns a project without clarifying key priorities and deadlines. The team works without clear direction, and the results fail to meet the manager's expectations. This creates tension: employees view the manager as ineffective, while the manager sees them as undisciplined and incompetent.

Tips for Improving Communication:

- Active Clarification: Employees can take the initiative to ask clarifying questions if instructions are unclear.
- Feedback: Suggest ways for the manager to improve communication within the team. For instance: "It would be helpful if you provided more detailed instructions at the start of the project."

- Listening Leaders: Effective managers not only give directives but also listen actively, ask clarifying questions, and acknowledge valuable ideas.

Practical Exercise:

- After your next meeting with your boss, write down how clear their instructions were.
- If something was unclear, make a list of questions to ask and seek clarification at the earliest opportunity.
- Try giving positive feedback to your boss when they communicate expectations clearly—this encourages them to continue developing this skill.

Brief Conclusion:
Communication is the foundation of effective team relationships. Gaps in communication lead to misunderstandings that can result in conflicts and misjudgments of a manager's competence. However, proactive employee efforts to seek clarification and provide open feedback can bridge these gaps and foster productive working relationships.

Methods for Evaluating Your Boss

Leadership Style Analysis: Daniel Goleman's Model of Emotional Intelligence Leadership.

Daniel Goleman, the author of the emotional intelligence concept, identifies six main leadership styles. Each style impacts the work environment differently, and understanding which style your boss uses can help you adjust your expectations and improve your interactions.

Six Leadership Styles by Goleman:

1. Authoritative (Visionary Leader).

- Focuses on inspiration and long-term vision.
- Useful when a new direction and motivation are needed.

Example: A boss emphasizes the future success of the company rather than current details.

2. Coaching.

- Concentrates on developing employees and their potential.
- Effective when the team needs support for growth.

Example: A manager holds regular meetings to discuss each employee's development goals.

3. Affiliative

- Creates an atmosphere of unity and belonging.
- Effective for fostering teamwork.

Example: A leader organizes informal gatherings to bond the team.

4. Democratic

- Involves employees in decision-making processes.
- Best when diverse opinions are valuable.

Example: A manager hosts brainstorming sessions to gather project ideas.

5. Pacesetting

- Focuses on high performance and a fast pace.
- Useful for tasks requiring quick execution but may lead to burnout.

Example: A boss demands tasks be completed quickly and sets high-quality standards.

6. Coercive (Authoritarian)

- Emphasizes discipline and control.
- Effective in crises requiring firm leadership.

Example: A manager closely monitors every project stage to meet deadlines.

Practical Application of Leadership Style Analysis.

- Step 1: Identify which style your boss uses most often. Observe their communication and decision-making approach.
- Step 2: Adjust your behavior. For instance, if your boss leans towards an authoritative style, follow instructions precisely and avoid unnecessary questions. If they use a democratic approach, contribute ideas, and engage in discussions.
- Step 3: Learn to find balance. If a leadership style presents challenges (e.g., micromanagement in a pacesetting style), discuss ways to improve communication or suggest alternative approaches.

Benefits of Analyzing Leadership Styles.

Understanding your manager's leadership style helps you adjust your expectations and reduce unnecessary stress. It also enables you to discover the most effective ways to work together, increasing your chances of team success. Goleman's model broadens your perception of leadership: even if your boss's style seems "wrong," it might be suitable in certain circumstances. The key is not only to understand the style but to be flexible and adapt to it.

Evaluating Your Boss's KPIs: Understanding Their Performance Metrics.

To work effectively with your boss, it's essential to understand the criteria by which their performance is measured. These criteria may differ significantly from your own views on what's important for successful task completion. By understanding your boss's goals and key performance indicators (KPIs), you can better interpret their decisions and actions.

What Are KPIs, and Why Are They Important?

KPIs (Key Performance Indicators) are measurable values that demonstrate how effectively business goals are being achieved. Managers are often evaluated on KPIs such as:

- Financial Results: Increasing profit, reducing costs, or growing revenue.
- Customer Satisfaction: Service quality and response time.
- Employee Productivity: Meeting project deadlines and maintaining engagement levels.

Understanding these indicators can help you interpret decisions that may seem irrational from your perspective.

Examples of KPIs Influencing Boss's Decisions:

1. Profit Increase:

If your boss focuses on profit growth, they might make decisions that sacrifice quality for cost-saving or faster market entry.

Example: Setting tight project deadlines to reduce labor costs, which may seem unreasonable to you.

2. Cost Reduction:

When budget optimization is a priority, your boss might cancel processes that seem important but are not critical.

Example: Skipping additional testing stages to cut costs may be justified from a budget standpoint.

3. Customer Satisfaction:

If the KPI centers on improving customer satisfaction, this could lead to decisions that prioritize service quality, even if they require extra resources.

Example: Investing in employee training, despite the expense, to retain clients long-term.

How to Evaluate Your Boss's KPIs?

- Step 1: Observe your boss's priorities. Which projects do they emphasize? What are their main goals?

- Step 2: Discuss expectations openly. Don't hesitate to ask questions about the goals set by upper management. This will help you understand how your work fits into the overall picture.
- Step 3: Look for connections. Understanding your boss's KPIs can help you align your efforts with their objectives, increasing your value as an employee.

Benefits of Understanding Your Boss's KPIs:

Knowing your manager's performance metrics not only enhances your understanding of their decisions but also helps you align your actions with their priorities. This can lead to better relationships and elevate your professional reputation within the team. Understanding your boss's KPIs is a key to more productive interactions and achieving shared goals.

Conclusion: Objective Perception as a Key to Better Relationships.

This chapter emphasized that perceiving a boss as "foolish" or incompetent is often a result of our own biases, priority differences, and mismatched management styles. Techniques like cognitive reframing and self-analysis can help you change your perspective and build more productive relationships with your manager.

Reflection on Growth

Instead of dwelling on disappointments, consider the situation as an opportunity for personal and professional growth: What can you learn from this experience? What skills can you develop in this environment? Such a mindset reduces stress and opens up new opportunities for career advancement.

For example, the ability to adapt to different management styles, recognize your own biases, and actively engage in communication can significantly improve your relationships with your boss. Taking the initiative, such as discussing priorities openly and seeking feedback, fosters a more transparent and effective work environment.

What's Next?

In the following chapters, we will explore specific strategies to improve interactions with management, even when it initially seems inefficient or problematic. You will learn methods to strengthen relationships with your boss and become a more valuable team member.

The journey toward understanding and collaboration is not just a path to professional success but also an opportunity for personal growth. By becoming aware of your reactions and biases, you can turn potential conflicts into opportunities to improve both your relationships and your professional skills.

Chapter 2: Empathy and Perspective-Taking

Empathy is a powerful force that bridges gaps between people, fostering understanding, compassion, and connection. In professional relationships—especially when dealing with a boss perceived as "incompetent"—empathy takes on heightened importance.

This chapter delves into the transformative power of empathy and perspective-taking, exploring how these qualities can improve workplace dynamics and enrich personal and professional growth.

Building empathy in the workplace is a key skill that allows individuals to form effective relationships, even with a manager who might evoke frustration.

Understanding your boss's perspective can shift how you perceive their decisions, reduce tension, and pave the way for more productive collaboration.

The Importance of Empathy.

Empathy is a critical skill that enables understanding and sharing the feelings and experiences of others. When working with a manager perceived as "incompetent" or challenging, empathy becomes an essential tool to overcome biases and build more productive relationships. Empathy helps individuals look beyond personal judgments, opening the door to deeper understanding and connection.

Understanding the Situation.

When a manager makes decisions that seem irrational or counterproductive, employees may be quick to dismiss their actions as foolish. However, taking the time to consider the manager's perspective—factoring in pressures from senior leadership or limited resources—can reveal valid reasons behind their choices.

Empathy as a Tool.

Using empathy in professional settings not only strengthens interpersonal relationships but also enhances team dynamics and satisfaction. Research shows that empathy in the workplace leads to higher levels of trust, fostering better collaboration and reducing conflicts (Cohen & Janicki, 2014).

Practical Application:

To cultivate empathy, employees can use the following approaches:

- Active Listening: Listen to your manager not merely to respond but to genuinely understand their perspective.
- Asking Questions: Clarify motivations and reasoning behind decisions to uncover the factors driving their actions.
- Practicing Compassion: Put yourself in your manager's shoes to better grasp their challenges and limitations.

Empathy in interactions with leadership can transform the dynamics of the relationship, making them more constructive and contributing to professional growth.

Developing Empathy for Your Boss's Position.

Leaders often operate under immense pressure, balancing demands from higher management, team expectations, and organizational goals. Recognizing that your boss may face challenges unknown to you—such as corporate constraints, tight deadlines, or personal struggles—can foster empathy.

Understanding the Role of Leadership.

Developing empathy for your boss requires deliberate effort to see the broader context of their decisions. For instance, a manager may face unexpected problems influencing their actions, such as budget cuts or new directives from senior executives.

The Skill of Active Listening.

One way to build empathy is through active listening, which involves not only hearing but also understanding the emotions and motivations behind the words. Approaching conversations with an open mind and genuine curiosity is essential.

- Ask Questions: Take time to ask clarifying questions and listen attentively to the answers. This helps uncover the rationale behind seemingly illogical decisions.
- Show Compassion: Try to imagine yourself in your boss's position. For example, if your manager abruptly changes project priorities, it could be due to directives from higher-ups rather than personal whims.

Creating a Foundation of Trust.

Demonstrating willingness to engage and empathize builds trust and respect, which are cornerstones of strong workplace relationships. This approach can lead to more effective communication and collaboration, ultimately benefiting the entire team.

Key Takeaway:

Developing empathy for your manager not only improves workplace relationships but also fosters a more supportive and productive work environment. Every decision has a context, and understanding this context can significantly enhance your perception of your boss.

Practicing Changing Perspective.

Beyond empathy, perspective-taking is a crucial skill for overcoming interpersonal challenges. This process involves putting yourself in another person's position and viewing the situation from their standpoint. It provides valuable insight into the factors shaping their thoughts, feelings, and behaviors.

Letting Go of Bias.

To effectively practice perspective-taking with your boss, start by releasing personal biases. Approach situations with an open mind, considering the challenges and pressures your leader may face both organizationally and personally. Reflect on questions such as:

- What factors might have influenced their decisions?
- What constraints or challenges are they experiencing at this stage?

Understanding Experience and Values.

Reflecting on your boss's past experiences, values, and motivations can offer insight into how these factors shape their actions. For instance, if your manager has a background in a fast-paced industry, their focus on meeting deadlines—even at the cost of process details—might stem from that experience.

Engaging in Meaningful Dialogue.

Seeking opportunities for meaningful dialogue with your manager—whether through one-on-one meetings, team discussions, or informal conversations—can further support perspective-taking. Active listening and validating their experiences demonstrate your willingness to understand and collaborate. This builds trust and mutual respect, creating a foundation for effective teamwork.

Tip: During discussions about projects or initiatives, ask open-ended questions to encourage your manager to share their thoughts and reasoning. This can lead to a deeper understanding of their approach and improve collaboration.

Key Takeaway:

Practicing perspective-taking not only enhances workplace relationships but also promotes a harmonious and productive work atmosphere. By considering your boss's viewpoint, you can better navigate challenges and foster conditions for successful collaboration.

The Method of "Realistic Empathy".

The method of realistic empathy focuses on understanding the logic behind your boss's actions, even when they seem irrational or unjustified.

This approach involves a deeper analysis of the situation to uncover the reasons behind your manager's decisions. Understanding these reasons can help reduce negative emotions and improve your working relationships.

Finding the Logic Behind Actions.

It's essential to remember that every decision has a basis, often influenced by external factors. For instance, if your boss decides to cut the budget for a project your team views as critical, it may be due to new financial plans the company must adhere to. In this case, the decision might be aimed at preventing larger losses rather than a lack of understanding of the team's needs.

Exercise for Practicing Realistic Empathy.

To apply the method effectively, try this exercise:

1. Situation Analysis: When you're upset by your boss's decision, ask yourself two key questions:

- "What does my boss know that I don't?"
- "What constraints might be influencing them?"

2. Write Down Your Thoughts: Note your answers and try to summarize any information that could explain their actions. This will help broaden your perspective and view the situation from their point of view.

Benefits of the Method.

Using the method of realistic empathy not only reduces stress and tension but also helps create a healthier work environment. Understanding your boss's motivations fosters mutual respect and trust, leading to more productive collaboration.

Thus, realistic empathy becomes a valuable tool for improving interactions with your manager, enabling you to better understand their actions and make more constructive decisions in challenging situations.

Evaluating and Gathering Feedback from Colleagues.

Feedback from colleagues can be a powerful tool for evaluating your boss's decisions and understanding their rationale. Often, when employees discuss work and management choices, they can uncover new aspects that may not have been noticed during individual analysis. This approach helps create a more comprehensive understanding of the situation.

Avoiding Gossip.

It's important to ensure that discussions about your boss's decisions remain constructive. Avoid gossip and negativity, as they can worsen perceptions of your manager and lead to further dissatisfaction. Instead, focus on objective evaluation.

Organizing Constructive Discussions.

Here are some tips for organizing discussions:

1. Team Meetings: Use team meetings as a platform for constructive dialogue. Rather than expressing frustration, ask

questions that can help you and your colleagues better understand the reasoning behind your boss's decisions. Examples of questions include:

- "Why do you think this decision was made?"
- "What potential benefits could this bring in the future?"

2. Forming a Balanced Opinion: Such discussions can help develop a more balanced view of management's actions and highlight positive aspects that may have been overlooked.

Benefits of Gathering Feedback.

Collecting feedback not only improves understanding but also strengthens team spirit. When employees discuss issues openly and honestly, it can increase trust within the team and improve overall workplace morale. Additionally, this practice may provide managers with insight into how their decisions are perceived at the team level, potentially leading to adjustments in the future.

Constructive Perception of Difficult Decisions

Developing empathy doesn't require fully agreeing with your boss's decisions but does help you understand their motives and create a constructive approach to working together. It's important to remember that seemingly irrational or complicated decisions often stem from circumstances that employees may not be aware of. This awareness can open the door to initiative and leadership qualities within the team.

Opportunities for Initiative.

When your boss implements a new rule or changes a process that seems difficult or inconvenient, try to view it as an opportunity rather than reacting with frustration or resistance. For example, if new rules make task approvals more complex, it may not be an indication of indifference but rather a necessity to adapt to new corporate requirements or constraints.

Showing Initiative.

Instead of simply complaining about the changes, consider how you can streamline processes for your team while still complying with the new rules. You could propose alternative procedures that meet the new requirements but make work more efficient and convenient for everyone. This approach not only demonstrates your understanding of the situation but also highlights your proactive attitude, which will be appreciated by both your boss and your colleagues.

Example:

Situation: Your boss introduces additional approval stages to increase project oversight.

Your Action: Instead of being upset, suggest creating templates or checklists to simplify the approval process. This will not only ease the workload but also show your proactive problem-solving approach.

This method can improve workflow and strengthen your relationship with management by demonstrating your willingness to work within changing conditions.

Overcoming Differences in Communication Styles.

One of the main challenges in interacting with a boss perceived as "foolish" is the difference in communication styles. What seems obvious to one person may be confusing or unclear to another, often leading to misunderstandings and conflicts. In such situations, empathy and perspective-taking become essential tools for bridging communication gaps and fostering effective dialogue.

Adapting to Your Boss's Communication Style.

When communicating with your manager, it's important to tailor your approach to their preferences. Some bosses prefer direct and concise communication, while others value detailed explanations and analysis.

Example: If your boss prefers brief, informative reports, avoid submitting long, complex documents. Instead, create short presentations or use visual aids to convey your ideas clearly.

Adapting your communication style not only enhances understanding but also shows respect for your boss's preferences, which can positively influence your working relationship.

Empathy and Understanding in Conflict Situations.

When misunderstandings or conflicts arise, it's helpful to approach the situation with empathy and an open mind. Instead of assigning blame or criticizing, try to understand the underlying reasons for the disconnect. This approach may include:

- Active Listening: Pay close attention to what your boss is saying, and ask clarifying questions to better understand their perspective.
- Collaborative Problem-Solving: Work together to find a mutually acceptable solution to the problem and overcome disagreements.

This mindset transforms potential obstacles into opportunities for growth and learning, benefiting both you and your boss. Approaching conflicts with a willingness to collaborate creates an atmosphere of trust and understanding, strengthening workplace relationships.

Brief Conclusion:

Differences in communication styles can pose significant challenges in professional relationships. However, they can be overcome with empathy, adaptability, and open dialogue. By applying these skills, you will not only improve your interactions with your boss but also foster a more productive and positive work environment.

Tips for Problem-Solving and Reducing Tension

1. Listen Actively: During conversations with your boss, avoid interrupting and ask for clarification if something is unclear. This demonstrates respect and a willingness to collaborate.
2. Ask Open-Ended Questions: Instead of expressing dissatisfaction, ask questions like, "What do you see as the priorities for this month?" or "What constraints influenced this decision?"
3. Seek Compromises: In challenging situations, suggest alternative solutions that consider the interests of both the team and your boss.
4. Maintain Open Dialogue: Regularly discussing expectations and goals helps align priorities and prevent misunderstandings.

Conclusion.

Empathy and the ability to see things, from another person's perspective, are not just soft skills but essential tools for reducing conflicts and improving the work environment. By developing these skills, employees can change how they perceive their boss and build more productive relationships. In the upcoming chapters, we will dive deeper into strategies for effective communication and learn how to build trust, even when it feels like your boss isn't always right.

Chapter 3: Effective Communication Strategies.

Clear and concise communication serves as the foundation of any successful relationship, especially within the fast-paced context of the workplace. When working with a boss perceived as "foolish," effective communication becomes even more crucial, offering a way to bridge differences in perspectives and facilitate understanding. This chapter explores practical strategies for enhancing communication skills, providing the tools needed to navigate complex interactions with your manager and ensure that your messages are accurately understood.

Understanding the Importance of Effective Communication.

Effective communication is more than just relaying information; it's about ensuring that the message is understood and interpreted as intended. In a workplace where people have varying levels of experience and expertise, clear communication is essential for promoting collaboration, preventing misunderstandings, and achieving organizational success.

For instance, if an employee receives vague instructions from their boss about a new project, the lack of clear guidance can lead to unmet expectations, causing frustration and tension within the team. In such situations, effective communication acts as a lifeline, allowing people to clarify expectations, seek feedback, and address any issues that arise.

Practical Tips for Improving Communication Skills.

Improving communication skills requires deliberate effort in developing key competencies, such as active listening, clarity, and confidence. By enhancing these skills, individuals can better articulate their thoughts and ideas, fostering meaningful dialogue and mutual understanding.

Clear and Concise Communication.

Clear and concise communication involves delivering information quickly and understandably, without unnecessary details or ambiguous language. It is especially important in situations where tasks require quick responses and precise execution. Vague instructions or too many irrelevant details can lead to misunderstandings, delays, and even errors. To prevent this, structured and clear communication is essential. One effective tool for organizing information is the SBAR method, which helps structure thoughts and convey information logically.

Detailed Overview of the SBAR Method.

The SBAR method (which stands for Situation, Background, Assessment, Recommendation) is a framework used for concise and clear communication, particularly in situations that require swiftly conveying the essence of an issue and proposing a solution. SBAR ensures that only the most important information is communicated in a logical order:

1. Situation: Start with a brief description of the current situation or problem. For example, "We are experiencing a delay in the delivery of materials for the project…"
2. Background: Provide context or reasons that led to this situation. This helps the listener understand the background of the issue. For example, "The delay occurred due to a supplier issue…"

3. Assessment: Share your assessment of the situation and outline any potential risks if no action is taken. This assessment highlights the urgency of the problem. For example, "We risk not completing the project on time…"
4. Recommendation: End with a specific suggestion for addressing the problem. This not only highlights the issue but also takes the first step toward a solution. For example, "I recommend contacting an alternative supplier…"

Benefits of the SBAR Method.

Using the SBAR method helps structure information and saves time in explaining a task. It is convenient for communicating with both management and colleagues, as it allows them to grasp the essence of the problem quickly and make decisions efficiently.

Applying the Method in Practice.

Thinking through potential solutions before discussing a problem with your boss increases your value as an employee, showing that you not only identify issues but also aim to provide solutions. For example, if a project is delayed due to resource problems, you could suggest options such as redistributing tasks or seeking additional suppliers.

Tip: Before approaching your boss, analyze the available options for solving the issue and prepare a couple of suggestions. This preparation minimizes the chance of further questions and enhances your credibility in problem-solving discussions.

By applying SBAR and preparing potential solutions, you can make communication more effective, thereby improving work processes and reducing team stress. Practicing structured communication not only enhances efficiency but also fosters a positive and productive working environment.

Avoiding Conflicts Through Clear Communication

Misunderstandings often occur due to the misinterpretation of words or intentions. Clarifying details and using active listening can help minimize these risks.

Active Listening.

Active listening involves fully engaging with the speaker and showing genuine interest in what they are saying. Research indicates that active listening not only enhances understanding but also builds trust and rapport (Barrios, 2016).

To practice active listening, focus entirely on the person speaking. Maintain eye contact and avoid interrupting or forming your response before they have finished. Instead, give them your full attention and listen intently. It is also helpful to paraphrase or summarize the key points to ensure you understand their message correctly.

Example of Ineffective Dialogue:
Boss: "I'd like to discuss the project deadline. Do you have a moment?"
Employee: "Sure."
Boss: "We need to make sure all tasks are completed by Friday. Can you confirm your team will meet the deadline?"
Employee: "Yeah, yeah, they'll manage."
Boss: "I need more than just assurances. Can you provide specific details on the progress and any potential obstacles?"
Employee: "Um, I think they're doing fine. There might be some issues, but nothing major."

In this scenario, the employee isn't listening carefully and responds vaguely, failing to provide concrete details or address potential obstacles.

Example of a Dialogue with Active Listening:
Boss: "I'd like to discuss the upcoming project. Do you have any thoughts or ideas?"
Employee: "Yes, I have a few suggestions. First, I think we should allocate more resources to the initial research phase to lay a solid foundation. Additionally, I've noticed some potential challenges with the timeline and would like to discuss strategies for addressing them."
Boss: "Thank you for your insights. Can you elaborate on the challenges you foresee with the timeline?"
Employee: "Of course. Based on our current projections, I'm concerned we may face delays due to the project's complexity. I think it would be beneficial to build in some flexibility to account for unforeseen circumstances."
Boss: "That's a valid concern. Let's review the timeline together and consider allocating additional resources if needed to ensure the project's success."

In this conversation, the employee actively listens and responds thoughtfully, offering specific examples to support their points. This approach leads to a productive discussion and collaborative problem-solving.

Clarity and Conciseness.

Clear and concise communication is essential for ensuring your message is understood correctly. Ambiguity or vague wording can lead to misunderstandings and confusion, particularly in the fast-paced work environment. Research indicates that using straightforward and simple language enhances understanding and reduces the likelihood of errors (Werner et al., 2018).

When communicating with your manager, make an effort to express your thoughts and ideas in a simple and direct manner. Avoid jargon or unclear language that may cause confusion.

Instead of relying on vague terms, use specific examples and relevant details to illustrate your points. Be prepared to provide additional explanations or context if needed to ensure your message is correctly interpreted.

Example of Ineffective Dialogue:

Boss: "Can you give me an update on the project budget?"

Employee: "Yes, it's a bit complicated. We've spent money on various things, but we're trying to keep it under control."

Boss: "I need a clear breakdown of expenses and how they align with the budget. Can you provide that?"

Employee: "I'll try, but it's kind of hard to explain."

In this scenario, the employee's response is unclear and vague, making it difficult for the boss to understand the current budget status.

Example of Dialogue with Clarity and Conciseness:

Boss: "I need an update on the status of the marketing campaign. Can you give me a brief overview?"

Employee: "Sure. The marketing campaign is set to launch next week. We've completed the creative materials, established partnerships with influencers, and scheduled social media posts for the launch. Overall, I'm confident we're well-prepared for a successful campaign."

Boss: "Thanks for the update. Can you elaborate on the social media strategy?"

Employee: "Of course. We've developed a content calendar detailing the timing and content of each social media post leading up to the launch. Additionally, we've identified key performance indicators to track the campaign's success and make any necessary adjustments."

In this example, the employee communicates with clarity and conciseness, providing a brief overview of the marketing campaign and offering specific details to support the update. This approach avoids unnecessary jargon and ensures the message is properly understood.

Assertive Communication.

Assertive communication involves expressing your thoughts, feelings, and opinions in a respectful and confident manner while also listening to and acknowledging the views of others. Research shows that assertive communication leads to more positive outcomes in interpersonal interactions, such as increased collaboration and mutual respect.

To practice assertive communication, use "I" statements to express your thoughts and feelings. Avoid passive or aggressive language and remain open to feedback and constructive criticism. Set clear boundaries and communicate your needs and expectations confidently and clearly.

Example of Ineffective Dialogue:

Boss: "I noticed you missed the project report deadline. Can you explain what happened?"

Employee: "Well, it's not entirely my fault. Some team members didn't finish their parts on time."

Boss: "I understand there may have been challenges, but I need you to take responsibility for your commitments. How do you plan to ensure this doesn't happen again?"

Employee: "I'll try, but I can't do much if others don't do their work."

In this dialogue, the employee is not communicating assertively, deflecting responsibility, and failing to provide a concrete plan for addressing the issue.

Example of Assertive Communication:

Boss: "I noticed you missed the project report deadline. What happened?"

Employee: "I encountered some challenges with the project that took more time than expected. I realize this affected the deadline, and I apologize. To prevent this in the future, I plan to notify you in advance if any delays seem likely."

Boss: "Thank you for being honest. It's important for me to be aware if something is off track. Can we discuss how to better monitor your progress?"

Employee: "Of course. I think regular status check-ins would help us stay aligned and address any issues early."

In this example, the employee uses assertive communication, taking responsibility for their actions and proposing a solution to avoid future problems. This approach fosters a more positive and productive dialogue, promoting cooperation and understanding between the boss and the employee.

Nonverbal Communication.

Nonverbal cues, such as facial expressions, body language, and tone of voice, play a crucial role in communication, often conveying more information than words alone. Research indicates that nonverbal communication significantly influences how a message is interpreted and how the communicator is perceived (Pease & Pease, 2017).

When communicating with your boss, be mindful of your nonverbal signals to ensure they align with your verbal message. Use open and positive body language, such as maintaining eye contact, facing the person you are speaking to, and nodding to show agreement. Additionally, pay attention to your tone of voice, as it can convey emotions and attitudes that may impact how your message is received.

Example of Ineffective Dialogue:

Boss: "I noticed you seemed irritated during the last meeting. Is something on your mind?"

Employee: (sighs) "It's just annoying dealing with all these problems."

Boss: "I understand, but it's important to remain professional and address your concerns directly. Can you explain what's bothering you?"

Employee: (shrugs) "Nothing specific. There's just a lot going on."

In this scenario, the employee's nonverbal cues, such as sighing and shrugging, convey irritation and disengagement, hindering effective communication with the boss.

Example of Effective Nonverbal Communication:

Boss: "I'd like to discuss the recent client meeting. How do you think it went?"

Employee: (maintains eye contact and nods) "Overall, I think the meeting went well. We addressed the client's concerns and presented our proposal effectively. However, there were a few moments when the client seemed unsure, and I believe we need to provide additional clarifications."

Boss: "I noticed you appeared confident during the presentation, but there were a few moments when you seemed uncertain. Can you elaborate on your observations?"

Employee: (uses open body language and gestures) "Sure. I noticed the client was particularly focused on our pricing structure. While I answered their questions, I think we can improve how we communicate our value proposition to potential clients."

In this dialogue, the employee uses effective nonverbal communication by maintaining eye contact, nodding to show understanding, and using open body language and gestures to convey confidence and engagement. Aligning nonverbal signals with the verbal message enhances clarity and impact, creating more effective and meaningful communication.

Seeking Feedback and Clarifications.

Effective communication is a two-way street that requires active participation from both sides in exchanging information. When communicating with your boss, seek feedback and ask for clarifications to ensure you understand their message correctly and that your message is being received as intended. Research shows that seeking feedback improves understanding and enhances the quality of communication (Riggs, 2019).

Be open to constructive criticism and willing to adjust your communication style or approach as needed to increase clarity and effectiveness. Additionally, take the initiative to ask for explanations on unclear or ambiguous points, and be ready to provide context or clarification to ensure mutual understanding.

Example of Ineffective Dialogue:

Boss: "I wanted to discuss the feedback you received on your presentation. Are there any areas where you think you could improve?"

Employee: "I'm not sure. I thought everything went fine."

Boss: "I appreciate your confidence, but there's always room for improvement. Can you reflect on the feedback and identify areas where you could make changes?"

Employee: "I guess I could, but I don't see the point. I thought it was fine."

In this example, the employee disregards the importance of seeking feedback and fails to recognize the potential for growth, hindering their professional development.

Example of a Dialogue Demonstrating Seeking Feedback and Clarifications:

Boss: "I wanted to discuss your work on the recent project. How do you think it went?"

Employee: "I appreciate the opportunity to discuss my work. Overall, I feel the project was successful, but I'm always looking for ways to improve. Are there any specific areas you think I could have handled better?"

Boss: "I thought you did an excellent job leading the team and meeting the project deadlines. However, there were a few instances where communication seemed to break down. Can you explain what happened?"

Employee: "Thank you for the feedback. I agree that communication was challenging at times. I think we could benefit from clearer expectations and more frequent check-ins to ensure alignment. Going forward, I'll make an effort to communicate more proactively and seek feedback to keep everyone on the same page."

In this example, the employee actively seeks feedback and clarifications from the boss, showing a willingness to reflect on their work and identify areas for improvement.

By engaging in an open and honest dialogue, the employee promotes a constructive feedback loop and supports continuous learning and growth.

Navigating Communication Challenges.

Despite our best efforts, communication difficulties and obstacles may arise, especially when dealing with a manager perceived as "foolish." In such situations, it is important to approach the situation with patience, empathy, and a willingness to collaborate.

Resolving Misunderstandings.

When misunderstandings occur, it's crucial to address them promptly and constructively. Instead of assigning blame or becoming defensive, aim to understand the root cause of the misunderstanding and work collaboratively with your boss to find a resolution. This may involve seeking clarifications, providing additional context or information, or adjusting your communication approach to ensure mutual understanding.

Example Dialogue:
Employee: "I wanted to discuss the feedback you provided on the project proposal. It seems there was some confusion regarding the project scope."
Boss: "I appreciate you bringing this to my attention. Can you clarify where the confusion occurred?"
Employee: "Of course. It seems there was a misunderstanding about the deliverables and project timeline. I'd like to discuss potential adjustments to make sure we're aligned moving forward.
Boss: "Thank you for pointing that out. Let's review the project requirements together and make any necessary corrections to ensure clarity and alignment."

In this dialogue, the employee addresses the misunderstanding proactively and constructively, focusing on finding a solution rather than assigning blame. By seeking clarification and working collaboratively, both the employee and the boss work toward a clearer, more productive outcome.

Developing Empathy.

In challenging communication situations, developing empathy toward your manager can foster understanding and maintain more positive interactions. Take the time to consider your manager's perspective, including their motivations, pressures, and constraints. Empathy can help you approach the situation with greater patience, compassion, and understanding.

Example Dialogue:
Employee: "I wanted to discuss the recent decision to adjust the project timeline. While I understand the importance of meeting deadlines, the shortened timeline has created some difficulties for our team."
Boss: "I hear your concerns. The decision to adjust the timeline was made to align with the company's strategic priorities and client expectations. I know it's challenging, but I believe we can work together to overcome these obstacles."
Employee: "Thank you for providing the context. I appreciate your perspective and I am willing to work on finding solutions to help us achieve our goals."

Seeking Support and Advice.
When facing communication challenges with a manager perceived as "foolish," don't hesitate to seek support and guidance from colleagues, mentors, or HR professionals. They may offer valuable insights, perspectives, or strategies for effectively addressing the situation. Additionally, consider seeking training or resources to improve your communication skills and ability to handle difficult interactions.

Example Dialogue:
Employee: "I've been having trouble communicating with our manager, and I'm not sure how to fix it. Do you have any advice or suggestions on how I can improve the situation?"
Colleague: "I've experienced similar issues before. One approach that might help is to schedule regular check-ins with your manager to openly discuss any concerns. It's also important to approach the situation with empathy and a willingness to collaborate."
Employee: "Thanks for the advice. I'll give that a try and see if it improves our communication."

If misunderstandings or conflicts arise, aim to address them promptly and constructively, focusing on finding solutions rather than assigning blame.

Use active listening and empathy to understand your manager's perspective and concerns, and strive to express your own thoughts and feelings clearly and confidently. Additionally, be open to feedback and willing to adjust your communication style or approach as needed to enhance clarity and effectiveness.

Constructive Communication for Conflict Resolution.

Constructive communication not only helps resolve conflicts but also prevents them from arising, fostering a team atmosphere of mutual respect and collaboration. To reduce tension and improve understanding, you can use the following proven approaches.

1. Avoid Blame with "I-Statements".

When communicating, it's essential to phrase your thoughts in a way that doesn't sound accusatory. Using "I-statements" instead of "you-statements" softens the tone of the conversation and reduces defensiveness. For instance, rather than saying, "You never send the reports on time," you could say, "I feel our project work would improve if we discussed deadlines and priorities in advance." This approach expresses your perspective without assigning blame, focusing on your experience rather than the other person's mistakes. It not only decreases the chances of escalating conflict but also encourages constructive dialogue.

Example of Using "I-Statements":
When facing criticism from a manager about the quality of a report, an employee might say: "I feel I need more specific instructions to meet your expectations." This statement addresses the misunderstanding without placing blame, paving the way for a collaborative solution.

2. Prepare Alternative Solutions.

It's crucial not just to point out problems, but also to suggest potential solutions. This demonstrates a positive attitude and a willingness to find compromises.

For example, if an employee feels the deadlines are too tight, they can suggest alternative ways to optimize the workflow or distribute the workload. Instead of simply stating, "These deadlines are unrealistic," it's more effective to say: "Could we consider redistributing tasks or bringing in additional resources?"

This proactive stance builds trust and shows a readiness to seek mutually beneficial solutions.

3. Hold Regular Check-Ins to Align Expectations.

Regular meetings and status updates can help identify issues early and prevent frustration from building up. Short check-ins or progress reports enable everyone to stay informed about changes and progress, aligning the expectations of both management and the team. Maintaining transparency through regular updates minimizes misunderstandings and keeps priorities in sync.

Example: If a manager assigns a task without clear success criteria, an employee can suggest a brief meeting to clarify the details.

During this meeting, discussing expectations and benchmarks can ensure both parties are on the same page, preventing future misunderstandings and disappointments.

Benefits of Constructive Communication.

Using these approaches reduces communication tension, fosters open dialogue, and creates an environment for productive feedback. This not only aids in conflict resolution but also strengthens professional relationships, building a culture of trust and respect within the team.

Evaluating Your Manager's Communication Style.

Evaluating your manager's communication style is a valuable tool for improving interactions and minimizing misunderstandings. Each manager has their own preferred ways of receiving information and may appreciate different approaches to reporting and communication. Understanding these preferences can help you adapt and effectively convey the necessary information.

Approaches to Evaluating Your Manager's Communication Style:

1. Identify Reporting Preferences:

Determine if your boss prefers detailed reports with extensive information or concise, high-level summaries. Some managers are results-oriented, and only want to see key takeaways, while others value transparency and a comprehensive breakdown of the process. If your manager prefers brevity, focus on the main points and avoid unnecessary details. Conversely, if they like to dive deep into the specifics, provide a more detailed account, supported by evidence and examples.

2. Observe Their Reactions to Different Types of Reports:

Experiment with varying levels of detail in your reports and observe your manager's response. If they respond briefly and without follow-up questions to a detailed report, they may prefer a more concise format. If they ask for further details or seek clarification, they likely appreciate a deeper level of analysis.

3. Seek Direct Feedback:

If your manager's preferences aren't immediately clear, politely ask them about their preferred format for reports or their communication style. This not only shows your willingness to adapt but also reassures them of your professionalism and commitment to effective communication.

4. Consider Communication Frequency:

Some managers prefer frequent updates on project progress, while others are more comfortable receiving comprehensive reports at the end of a project phase. Determine the preferred frequency and adjust accordingly, ensuring that you neither overwhelm them with information nor leave them uninformed.

Example:

- If your manager prefers concise summaries, start your report with the main findings, key metrics, and recommendations. Use bullet points or tables for clarity and quick comprehension.
- If they appreciate detailed information, structure the report into sections that include the task description, methodology, results, and conclusions. Ensure easy access to data by including links to sources or appendices.

Benefits of Adapting to Your Manager's Communication Style.

Tailoring your communication style not only enhances the efficiency of interactions but also demonstrates your flexibility and professionalism to your manager. This approach helps prevent misunderstandings and fosters trust, making your work more productive and creating a more harmonious work environment.

Conclusion.

Overcoming communication challenges with a manager perceived as "foolish" requires patience, empathy, and effective communication strategies. Active listening, assertive communication, and seeking feedback and clarifications can help resolve misunderstandings, foster mutual understanding, and promote positive interactions with your manager. Additionally, developing empathy and seeking support from colleagues or mentors can aid in handling difficult situations and contribute to a more collaborative and productive work environment.

Clear and structured communication is key to successful interactions with your manager. Utilizing active listening, the SBAR method, and a constructive approach to discussing issues can prevent conflicts and build trust within the workplace. In the next chapter, we will explore how to establish trust with leadership and strengthen collaboration, turning workplace challenges into opportunities for growth.

Chapter 4: Building Trust and Understanding

Trust is the foundation of any meaningful relationship, and the professional relationship between an employee and their manager is no exception. In this chapter, we will dive into the complex process of building trust and understanding with your manager.

Drawing on real-world examples, scientific research, and historical insights, we will explore key principles and strategies that can help strengthen trust and foster strong working relationships.

Understanding Trust.

Trust is a multifaceted concept that encompasses reliability, integrity, and mutual respect. It is built through consistent actions and behaviors that demonstrate dependability and honesty. Organizational psychology research shows that trust is essential for fostering collaboration, communication, and engagement in the workplace (Dirks & Ferrin, 2002).

Principles of Building Trust.

Building trust with your manager requires deliberate effort and commitment to certain principles:

1. Reliability: Consistency is key to building trust. Be dependable and consistent in your actions and commitments. Fulfill your promises and meet deadlines. By demonstrating reliability, you show your manager that they can count on you.
2. Integrity: Integrity forms the foundation of trust. Be honest, ethical, and transparent in your interactions with your manager. Acknowledge mistakes when they occur and take responsibility for your actions. By embodying integrity, you establish yourself as a trustworthy and dependable team member.

3. Open Communication: Effective communication is crucial for building trust. Be open, honest, and transparent in your communication with your manager. Proactively share relevant information and updates, and be receptive to feedback and suggestions. Creating open lines of communication fosters a culture of trust and collaboration.
4. Empathy: Empathy is the ability to understand and share the feelings of others. Show empathy toward your manager by striving to understand their perspective, challenges, and concerns. Actively listen to their feedback and worries, and offer support and assistance when needed. Demonstrating empathy builds mutual understanding and strengthens your relationship with your manager.

Scientific Basis.

Research in organizational psychology provides valuable insights into the dynamics of building trust in the workplace. Studies indicate that trust is influenced by factors such as perceived benevolence, integrity, and competence (Dirks & Ferrin, 2002). By embodying these qualities in your interactions with your manager, you can cultivate trust and understanding over time.

Historical Insights.

Throughout history, trust has played a key role in shaping leadership and interpersonal relationships. Leaders such as Abraham Lincoln, Mahatma Gandhi, and Nelson Mandela were known for their unwavering integrity, honesty, and commitment to their principles. Their ability to inspire trust and build understanding with their followers enabled them to lead effectively and achieve significant social change.

Brief Conclusion:

Building trust and understanding with your manager is essential for creating a positive and productive work environment. By embodying the principles of reliability, integrity, open communication, and empathy, you can foster trust and develop strong working relationships. Drawing on insights from real-world examples, scientific research, and historical perspectives, you can confidently navigate the complexities of workplace interactions. Trust is not built overnight, but with patience, effort, and a sincere commitment to mutual success, you can lay the foundation for a trusting and mutually beneficial relationship with your manager.

Methods for Building Trust.

Building trust in professional relationships requires discipline, time, and consistency. Trust with your manager, in particular, is crucial for a comfortable work atmosphere and career advancement. Let's take a closer look at key approaches to strengthening trust.

1. Perform High-Quality Work

Professionalism and competence are foundational elements of trust. Consistently delivering high-quality work on time and with minimal errors demonstrates your reliability to your manager. It's important not only to complete assignments but also to strive for continuous improvement. Here are a few steps:

- Maintain and enhance your skills: Continuously upgrade your knowledge and skills to remain a valuable and up-to-date professional.
- Check your work for quality: Before submitting any work, review it carefully to correct errors and polish details. This shows that you aim to meet or exceed expectations.
- Anticipate potential problems: If a project or task risks delays or mistakes, inform your manager in advance. This creates a reputation of being a proactive and dependable employee.

2. Avoid Gossip and Demonstrate Loyalty

Loyalty and steering clear of gossip are also crucial in building trusting relationships. Criticizing your manager or colleagues can damage trust and negatively impact your reputation:

- Do not participate in negative conversations: Even if discussing management is common practice in your workplace, avoid engaging in such discussions. Focus instead on solutions and productive work.
- Offer constructive feedback: If you have concerns about your manager's decisions or actions, communicate them directly and constructively, suggesting alternatives or explaining your perspective. For example, you might say: "I understand that the chosen approach is effective in the short term, but I'd like to suggest some options that could also benefit us long term."
- Support your manager and the company during difficult times: During crises or periods of significant change, show your willingness to adapt and find solutions to overcome challenges. This demonstrates that you care not just about your interests, but also about the company's and team's well-being.

These methods help create the image of an employee who is trustworthy and who maintains stability and order in the workplace. By adopting this approach, you can gradually strengthen your manager's trust and establish yourself as a responsible and loyal professional.

Mutual Respect as a Key Element.

Mutual respect is essential for successful professional relationships and a harmonious work environment. Treating your manager and their decisions with respect, while also expressing your opinions constructively, helps foster trust and prevent conflicts. Here's how to apply mutual respect in practice:

1. Respect Your Manager's Time.

Understanding and respecting your manager's time constraints contribute to more productive communication:

- Schedule meetings with consideration: Before suggesting a meeting, check your manager's availability to avoid conflicts and show thoughtfulness.
- Be prepared: When discussing specific issues, come with a brief summary and key questions. This ensures meetings are efficient and to the point. For example, if you need to discuss project progress, compile relevant data and key points to quickly explain the current status and potential challenges.
- Consider alternatives: If an in-person meeting isn't feasible, think about other ways to communicate, such as via email or messaging apps. This flexibility demonstrates respect for your manager's time.

2. Constructive Disagreement.

If you have a different opinion, it's important to express it respectfully and constructively:

- Use facts and data: When you disagree with a decision, focus on objective information. For instance, if you believe a certain decision may negatively impact a project, back up your opinion with specific data. This makes your disagreement more professional and persuasive.
- Offer solutions: Instead of just expressing disagreement, suggest alternative approaches. For example, you could say: "I understand why this approach was chosen, but perhaps we could consider another option that might achieve the same results with fewer resources."
- Maintain a respectful tone: Remember, the goal is to find the best solution, not to win an argument. Focus on the shared objective and use respectful language to support a constructive conversation.

These practices help create a healthy and productive work environment where team members can share their perspectives openly while maintaining mutual respect.

Examples and Tips for Problem-Solving.

Here are some examples and practical tips for handling difficult situations with your manager, enabling you to express your views and propose constructive alternatives:

Example 1: Offering an Alternative Solution When Disagreeing.

Situation: Your manager decides to significantly cut the budget for a project you are involved in, which raises concerns about the quality of execution.

Your Actions:

1. Listen Carefully: Start by listening to your manager's rationale. Understanding their reasoning will help you better articulate your concerns.
2. Express Concern and Propose Alternatives: Instead of directly expressing dissatisfaction, you might say:

"I understand why we need to reconsider the budget, but I'm worried this could impact the final outcome. May I suggest a few cost-saving measures that could help maintain quality without additional expenses?"

This approach demonstrates understanding and respect for your manager's decision while offering productive solutions, showing your willingness to collaborate and problem-solve.

Example 2: Active Listening and Clarifying Details.

Situation: Your manager sets deadlines that seem unrealistic for completing a task.

Your Actions:

1. Practice Active Listening: Pay close attention to your manager's explanation, focusing on their expectations and the reasons behind the tight deadlines.
2. Ask Clarifying Questions: Seek to clarify the details with questions such as:

"Am I correct in understanding that the primary goal is to meet the deadline, even if it means bringing in additional support or reallocating tasks?"

This question helps clarify expectations and opens the door to discussing solutions. Tip: Focus on discussing how to achieve the goal rather than emphasizing the impossibility of meeting the deadline. This reflects professionalism and a willingness to cooperate.

Example 3: Clarifying Expectations to Prevent Misunderstandings.

Situation: Your manager gives you an assignment without clear criteria for success.

Your Actions:

1. Prepare for the Discussion: Draft a few questions that will help clarify what is expected.

2. Request a Meeting to Discuss Goals: For instance, you could say:

"I'd like to ensure we're on the same page. Could we discuss the project's specific goals and which outcomes are most important?"

This approach not only helps prevent misunderstandings but also demonstrates your professionalism and commitment to quality.

Useful Tips for Constructive Problem-Solving.

- Practice Active Listening: Active listening shows respect for your manager and helps you better understand their perspective. Paraphrase their words to confirm your understanding. For example, say:

"If I understand correctly, the main objective is to…" Evaluate Your Manager's Communication Style: Knowing your manager's preferred communication style helps tailor your approach. If they prefer brevity, focus on concise conclusions and recommendations. If they value detail, provide context and evidence to support your ideas.

- Prepare Alternative Solutions: When identifying a problem, present multiple solutions. This shows your readiness to collaborate and contribute to the team's goals.
- Maintain Mutual Respect: When you disagree, frame your critique as suggestions and ideas rather than outright opposition. For example:

"Let's consider a few approaches that might help us achieve our goal more effectively."

These strategies will foster open and respectful interactions, encourage problem resolution, and strengthen trust between you and your manager.

The following examples illustrate both the lack of trust at a workplace, and the negative impact it can have. They emphasize the crucial role trust plays in organizational success, employee well-being, and overall productivity.

1. Fear-Based Culture: Some companies foster a culture of fear, where employees feel apprehensive about sharing their thoughts and ideas. A notable case is Uber in 2017, when reports of a toxic work environment and lack of trust between management and employees emerged. The situation led to the resignation of CEO Travis Kalanick and significant cultural shifts, as employees did not feel safe raising concerns or reporting problems. (Source: The New York Times)
2. Lack of Feedback: Organizations that lack open dialogue suffer from eroded trust. For instance, in 2016, Wells Fargo was embroiled in a scandal involving the creation of millions of fake accounts. Employees were too afraid to report issues due to the

risk of being fired, resulting in a massive loss of trust among customers and a damaged company reputation. (Source: Bloomberg)
3. Ignoring Employee Input: When leadership dismisses employee opinions or fails to consider their suggestions, trust breaks down. An example is General Motors, where, after a 2014 factory incident linked to car defects, it was revealed that many employees had raised safety concerns that were ignored. This led to significant financial losses and a decline in consumer trust. (Source: The Washington Post)

These cases highlight how a lack of trust can lead to severe organizational consequences, such as reduced productivity, reputational damage, and high employee turnover.

Now these are examples of successful implemetation of trust-building methodology, that can serve as an inspiration:

1. Google's Culture of Openness: Google provides numerous examples of how a culture of trust and transparency enhances productivity. Through their "Project Aristotle" initiative, Google found that teams with high levels of trust handled conflicts better and achieved superior results. By encouraging openness and honest problem-solving discussions, Google fosters mutual respect and trust between employees and management.
2. Patrick Lencioni's Trust Model: Patrick Lencioni, in his book The Five Dysfunctions of a Team, emphasizes the importance of trust as the foundation for effective teamwork. He advocates for open discussions of weaknesses and vulnerabilities among team members. Companies that implement his methods report improved collaboration and healthier work environments. For example, organizations following his principles adopt practices that promote transparency, resulting in higher performance and better team dynamics.
3. IBM's "Speak Up" Initiative: IBM developed a change management strategy focused on building trust between leadership and employees. Their "Speak Up" program encourages staff to share concerns and ideas through safe, structured channels. This approach has not only improved workplace morale but also allowed leadership to address employee needs more effectively.

These success stories demonstrate how trust and understanding can positively impact workplace relationships and overall performance. For further exploration, resources such as Harvard Business Review articles and Gallup research offer in-depth insights into trust-building practices.

Conclusion.

In conclusion, it is important to emphasize the importance of patience, consistency, and sincerity in building trusting relationships with your manager. These efforts are worthwhile, creating a work environment where interactions become more open and productive. Showing respect for your manager, striving for mutual understanding, and being willing to support their decisions or offer constructive alternatives help establish you as a valuable employee.

When you respect your manager's time, opinions, and preferences and uphold high standards of professionalism, you lay the foundation for mutual respect and trust. This trust fosters better communication and reduces tension, making the work process more efficient and harmonious for the entire team.

Building these relationships takes time and patience, but in the long run, they yield significant benefits for both your career and team dynamics.

Chapter 5: Finding Opportunities in Difficult Situations.

Challenging workplace scenarios, particularly when dealing with a manager perceived as "foolish," can initially seem daunting. However, it is essential to recognize that such difficulties often harbor opportunities for growth and development. This chapter explores how to reframe adversities as catalysts for personal and professional advancement, turning obstacles into stepping stones for success.

Understanding Adversity.

Understanding adversity involves acknowledging its inevitability and appreciating its role in our lives. It requires shifting the perception of hardships from purely negative experiences to valuable lessons in personal growth. Adversity takes many forms, ranging from personal setbacks and conflicts to external challenges like financial crises or unforeseen life changes.

Adversity as a Universal Experience.

Adversity is an integral part of life, experienced by everyone at some point. Recognizing this universality helps mitigate self-criticism and supports emotional resilience. Challenges are not unique manifestations of personal shortcomings but rather a natural part of human existence.

The Role of Perception in Facing Adversity.

Research shows that how we perceive adversity significantly impacts our ability to cope with it. Viewing challenges as opportunities rather than threats activates constructive coping strategies. Individuals with a growth mindset see difficulties as chances to learn and adapt, fostering resilience and self-confidence.

Adversity and Personal Growth.

Difficult times often spur personal growth, enhancing creativity and problem-solving abilities. Psychological studies suggest that stressful situations can motivate individuals to seek innovative solutions and explore new approaches. This process not only resolves specific issues but also strengthens one's capacity to handle future challenges.

Insights into Understanding Adversity.

Constructively approaching adversity requires recognizing and processing emotions. Techniques such as journaling, self-reflection, or confiding in trusted individuals can help. These practices deepen understanding of personal reactions to hardships and reveal opportunities for learning.

By acknowledging the inevitability of adversity and leveraging it for development, challenges can transform from sources of stress into powerful tools for growth.

Discovering Hidden Opportunities.

Dealing with a difficult manager may feel like an insurmountable challenge, but such situations often contain hidden opportunities for personal and professional development. Overcoming difficulties can lead to the cultivation of valuable skills such as flexibility, creativity, and resilience.

Strategies for Leveraging Challenges.

1. Adopting a Growth Mindset.

A growth mindset encourages seeing obstacles and setbacks as opportunities to learn and develop. This perspective helps you view challenges not as barriers to success, but as a means to enhance your skills. Research shows that individuals with a growth mindset, who perceive failures as temporary and solvable, recover from difficulties faster and achieve greater long-term success.

For example, when faced with criticism from your manager, instead of taking it as a personal affront, you can interpret it as valuable feedback to refine your skills and approaches. This mindset shifts the focus from defensiveness to proactive improvement.

2. Identifying Areas for Development.

Analyzing challenges can uncover opportunities for personal and professional growth. Difficulties in interacting with a manager might reveal areas for improvement, such as communication, leadership, or time management.

Ask yourself:

"What skills do I need to enhance to improve this interaction?"

"What steps can I take to handle these tasks more effectively?"

By addressing these questions, you not only overcome immediate issues but also set the stage for ongoing self-improvement.

3. Seeking Feedback and Support.

Feedback is a powerful tool that can help you identify areas of your behavior or work that require improvement. Actively seeking feedback from colleagues, mentors, or even your manager is essential for professional growth. Soliciting advice or recommendations allows you to gain insight into how you can enhance your performance and team interactions. Often, an external perspective can provide valuable clarity, helping you recognize issues from a different angle and discover solutions you may not have considered.

4. Maintaining Resilience.

Resilience is the ability not only to overcome difficulties but also to recover from them. To achieve this, it is important to maintain a positive attitude even when everything seems challenging. Practices aimed at improving resilience include focusing on solutions rather than problems, maintaining a balance between work and rest, and seeking support from colleagues and friends. The goal is not to avoid failures, but to learn how to cope with them and use them as fuel for growth.

Key Takeaway:

Turning challenges into catalysts for growth requires deliberate effort and self-reflection. By adopting a growth mindset, identifying opportunities for development, seeking feedback, and building resilience, you can transform difficulties into stepping stones toward achieving personal and professional goals. These strategies not only help you navigate adversity but also position you for success in future endeavors.

Scientific Foundation.

Research in positive psychology has identified resilience as a critical factor for overcoming adversity and achieving success. Studies show that individuals with a growth mindset—those who perceive challenges as opportunities for growth—are more likely to persist and thrive despite hardships.

When facing difficulties, your approach to problem-solving can make a significant difference. Let's examine how you can leverage challenging situations to foster personal and professional growth:

1. Flexibility.

Flexibility in problem-solving is the ability to adapt to changes and new circumstances. When working with a difficult manager, it is important to understand that their management style and requirements may shift depending on the situation. For instance, if your manager prefers concise reports over lengthy, detailed ones, it might be due to their workload or a need for efficiency. To meet such demands, it is essential to communicate information clearly, highlight key points, and quickly formulate conclusions. This not only helps meet expectations but also enhances efficiency in dynamic conditions.

Practical steps: Try adapting your work style. For example, if you previously wrote lengthy reports with detailed explanations, consider making them shorter, focusing on key points, and using bullet points for clarity.

2. Creativity.

Creativity helps go beyond standard solutions and propose unconventional approaches to problem-solving. This is particularly important in complex situations where traditional methods do not work or fail to achieve the desired outcome. For instance, if your manager does not respond well to standard reports or proposals, consider using visual materials or interactive methods—charts, infographics, or presentations with dynamic elements. This can not only capture their attention but also make the information easier to comprehend by presenting it in a more engaging and accessible way.

Practical steps: Use various formats to present information: interactive presentations, diagrams, mind maps, or even simple graphs to support your ideas and proposals. This approach can also demonstrate your flexibility and willingness to adapt.

3. Stress Resilience.

Stress resilience is the ability to maintain clarity of thought and work effectively even when the situation demands quick responses or feels overwhelming. When working with a difficult manager or on challenging projects, the ability to manage stress can be a critical factor for success. One way to handle stress is through breathing exercises, which help to calm the mind and regain focus. Additionally, meditation and relaxation techniques can be beneficial for restoring balance and energy during tense moments.

Practical steps: Use breathing exercises, such as the 4-7-8 deep breathing technique, to calm yourself and regain focus. You can also practice short meditations to reduce stress during the workday. These practices will not only improve your emotional state but also enhance your productivity and ability to make balanced decisions.

Key Takeaways:

When facing challenges, applying flexibility, creativity, and stress resilience not only helps address current problems but also fosters the development of personal and professional skills, which, in the long term, improves workplace relationships and contributes to career growth.

Learning from Mistakes.

One of the most effective ways to grow is by analyzing mistakes and problematic situations. Documenting and evaluating failures can significantly enhance your competence.

1. Analyzing Mistakes

Mistake analysis is a cornerstone of self-improvement.
Keeping track of errors and their circumstances allows you to identify patterns and areas for growth. By maintaining a journal, you can document key aspects: when the error occurred, what triggered it, the actions you took, and your manager's response. Over time, this record can highlight recurring issues and guide corrective actions.

Practical Example:
Imagine you failed to convey your ideas effectively during a meeting, leading to confusion among colleagues. Write down what caused this—perhaps insufficient preparation or information overload. Reflect on how you could have approached the situation differently, such as organizing your points in advance and preparing a concise summary.

Tip:
Regularly reviewing your mistakes can boost self-awareness, reduce the likelihood of repetition, and increase confidence in decision-making.

2. Seeking Feedback.

Feedback is essential for growth. Discussing your mistakes with colleagues or mentors provides fresh perspectives and practical advice. Their input can help you refine your approach and develop preventive strategies. Experienced mentors can share valuable insights based on their expertise, accelerating your learning curve and reducing future risks.

Practical Example:
After making a mistake in a report, approach a colleague or your manager and ask, "How would you have handled this situation?" or "What changes do you suggest for next time?" This demonstrates your openness to improvement and fosters a collaborative atmosphere.

Tip:

Embracing constructive criticism and actively listening to feedback will align your work more closely with expectations, enhancing your performance and workplace relationships.

3. The "What If" Exercise.

Once you've analyzed a mistake, conduct a "what if" exercise.

Reimagine the situation with alternative actions based on what you've learned. This practice sharpens your problem-solving skills, improves your ability to react swiftly, and helps develop contingency plans for similar challenges in the future.

Practical Example:

If a past project was delayed because you didn't start preparing the report early enough, ask yourself, "What if I had allocated an hour each day for this task earlier in the timeline?" This reflection might lead to creating a more proactive schedule for upcoming projects.

Tip:

Regularly practicing the "what if" exercise enhances forecasting abilities and decision-making, preparing you to navigate complex situations more effectively.

Key Takeaway:

Analyzing mistakes, seeking feedback, and applying the "what if" exercise are powerful tools for self-improvement.

Understanding that errors are not the end, but rather opportunities for learning, enables you to build confidence and competence in your professional life. Adopting these strategies transforms challenges into valuable experiences, helping you grow into a more effective and adaptable professional.

Real Life Examples:

- Eric Schmidt, former CEO of Google, encountered numerous critical moments in his career. Instead of viewing them as failures, he saw them as opportunities for learning and growth, implementing new strategies and management approaches.
- Melinda Gates has also shared her lessons from challenging work situations. She notes that difficulties along the way can inspire creative solutions, ultimately leading to successful projects.

Problem-Solving Tips.

1. The "First Step" Approach One key method for problem-solving is taking the first step. Difficult situations often feel overwhelming or complicated, leading to procrastination or delayed decision-making. However, taking even a small action can yield significant results. This could range from a simple conversation with a colleague or manager to drafting an action

plan. This approach helps reduce stress and brings clarity to the situation. Often, solving a problem begins with small yet decisive steps.

Example: If a project is delayed, the first step could be creating a list of tasks that need completion and allocating resources to execute them. This reduces uncertainty and initiates progress.

2. Networking and Collaboration

Support from colleagues and professionals in your network can play a crucial role in addressing difficult situations. Networking allows for sharing experiences and gaining new ideas for problem-solving. Often, someone in your network has faced similar challenges and can offer tried-and-true solutions or unique approaches.

Furthermore, support from colleagues and mentors strengthens professional connections and can contribute to career advancement. Even a simple discussion with experienced colleagues can provide fresh perspectives and better solutions.

Example: If you're struggling with a project, discuss it with colleagues, seek advice, or consult a more experienced specialist. Sharing insights may provide a valuable perspective you hadn't considered.

3. Continuous Learning and Development

Never stop investing in your learning and development. Solving problems often requires new knowledge or skills that help you tackle challenges effectively. Education doesn't end with a degree or completing a course; continuous improvement is essential. Applying new knowledge in practice enhances adaptability and problem-solving skills.

Consider enrolling in courses, seminars, or training sessions to develop the competencies you need. This can also include building soft skills, such as time management, resilience, or communication abilities.

Example: If you're struggling with project management, consider taking training in project management methodologies (e.g., Agile, Scrum or other). This will provide you with tools to improve workflows and optimize tasks.

Each of these approaches enhances your problem-solving abilities and serves as a crucial component in overcoming challenges successfully. Applying these strategies helps you tackle obstacles more effectively and confidently.

Conclusion.

Challenging situations with a boss perceived as "foolish" may seem overwhelming at first glance, but they also provide opportunities for growth, learning, and development. By adopting a growth mindset, identifying areas for improvement, seeking feedback and support, and building resilience, individuals can use difficulties as a catalyst for personal and professional advancement. Through analyzing mistakes, exploring new approaches, and committing to continuous self-improvement, you can transform challenges into opportunities. By embracing challenges and learning lessons from every situation, you can build a successful career and grow as a person. Remember, hardships are not barriers, but rather stepping stones to success. Embrace challenges, learn from setbacks, and continue striving for excellence in everything you do.

Chapter 6: Self-Care and Well-Being.

Self-care encompasses a wide range of actions and practices aimed at improving overall well-being and maintaining balance in life.

This includes proactive steps to care for one's physical, emotional, and mental health, ensuring the energy and resilience needed to overcome the challenges of work and life.

Psychological research demonstrates that self-care practices offer numerous benefits, including stress reduction, mood enhancement, increased productivity, and an overall improved quality of life (Rebar et al., 2015).

By prioritizing self-care, individuals can build resilience and better manage the challenges they face in the workplace.

Managing Stress and Emotional Burnout.

Stress and emotional burnout in the workplace can have long-term effects on both physical and mental health. It is crucial to actively address these states by utilizing proven methods. Below are several strategies to effectively manage stress and avoid burnout.

Relaxation Techniques.

Deep Breathing: One of the simplest and most effective ways to manage stress is through deep breathing. Research indicates that deep breathing can significantly reduce stress levels by slowing the heart rate and relaxing the muscles. Practicing deep breaths and exhales can refocus your attention on your breathing, reduce anxiety, and bring your awareness to the present moment.

Meditation: Meditation is a powerful tool that helps reduce stress levels and build resilience against it. Regular meditation practice improves emotional well-being, enhances focus, and reduces symptoms of anxiety and depression. For instance, studies show that meditation activates brain areas related to emotion regulation and decision-making (Rebar et al., 2015). Starting with short sessions of 10–15 minutes a day can be highly effective.

Yoga: Yoga combines physical exercises with meditation and breathing techniques, helping to relax both the body and the mind. It reduces stress, improves physical condition, and promotes inner peace. Regular yoga sessions can improve sleep quality and alleviate chronic stress.

Resting Routine and Hobbies.

Maintaining a Resting Routine:

Effective stress management is impossible without adequate rest. Overwork and the lack of recovery time only exacerbate stress responses and can lead to burnout. Prioritizing quality sleep, relaxation, and downtime is essential for maintaining overall well-being.

Engaging in Hobbies:

Participating in enjoyable activities, such as drawing, music, sports, or crafts, can be an excellent way to distract from work concerns. These activities not only help relieve tension but also restore emotional balance. They can also serve as an outlet for emotions and a means of coping with internal pressure.

Connecting with Loved Ones:

Support from friends and family plays an important role in combating burnout. Interacting with loved ones helps strengthen social bonds, create emotional support, and reduce stress levels. Care and attention from those around you can be key to regaining inner balance.

Key Takeaway:

Managing stress and emotional burnout requires a comprehensive approach that includes regular relaxation practices, maintaining a rest routine, and actively engaging in enjoyable hobbies. These methods not only help address current stress but also establish a foundation for long-term emotional well-being.

Maintaining Work-Life Balance.

Maintaining a balance between work and personal life is essential for long-term well-being and productivity. When this balance is disrupted, it can lead to issues with physical and emotional health, as well as a decline in the quality of work and relationships.

Setting Boundaries.

Clear boundaries between work and personal life form the foundation for a healthy balance. Establishing such boundaries helps prevent burnout and makes time for relaxation more effective. Here are several key aspects:

Defining Work Hours:

One of the first steps is to determine exactly when your workday starts and ends. Set clear working hours and stick to them. This helps avoid the feeling that work "never ends." For example, if your workday ends at 6:00 PM, try not to respond to work emails or tasks after that time unless it's critically important.

Using Calendars and Planners:

Planning not only helps organize your time better but also allows you to schedule "downtime." Use a calendar to log work tasks as well as personal time. Scheduling both work and leisure ensures you don't overburden yourself. For instance, digital tools like Google Calendar can help synchronize work meetings with personal events, reserving time for rest and hobbies.

Disconnecting from Work After Hours:

After work, make a conscious effort to physically and mentally "unplug" from your job. This can include practices like turning off work phones or software to avoid the temptation of continuing to work.

Creating Space for Personal Life:

It's essential to protect your personal space from constant work-related interruptions. This is especially important if you work remotely. Setting up a dedicated workspace at home or defining separate areas for rest and work can help maintain a healthy balance.

Benefits of Setting Boundaries

Burnout Prevention:

Regular rest and recovery reduce the risk of burnout. Without a clear separation between work and personal life, you may overwork yourself and lose motivation.

Improved Physical and Emotional Health:

Setting boundaries helps you manage stress more effectively, avoid chronic fatigue and anxiety, and improve overall well-being.

Increased Productivity:

Taking time to recharge enhances focus and efficiency at work. Rest periods allow you to tackle tasks with greater concentration and effectiveness.

Ultimately, setting boundaries between work and personal life fosters harmony and helps you avoid overexertion. This balance contributes to better health, stronger relationships, and improved performance in all areas of life.

Practical Examples:

Arianna Huffington: As the co-founder and former editor-in-chief of The Huffington Post, Arianna Huffington experienced firsthand the toll that stress and burnout can take on health and well-being. After collapsing from exhaustion and lack of sleep, Huffington made self-care a priority in her life. She incorporated practices such as mindfulness, meditation, and adequate sleep into her daily routine, which significantly improved her health, well-being, and productivity.

Richard Branson: As the founder of Virgin Group, Richard Branson leads a demanding and fast-paced lifestyle. Despite his busy schedule, Branson prioritizes self-care and well-being, recognizing the importance of maintaining balance in his life. He makes time for regular physical activity, rest, and connecting with loved ones, which he credits as contributing factors to his long-lasting success and career longevity.

Similarly, many companies have started implementing flexible work policies, allowing employees to allocate time for personal life, ultimately enhancing job satisfaction and reducing stress levels.

Tips for Problem-Solving.

Here are additional tips for effectively managing issues related to work-life balance:

1. Record Your Achievements.

When work tasks start consuming all your time, it's important to remember what you've already accomplished. Keeping a success journal can help you recognize your achievements and boost your morale. Writing down even small wins reduces stress and increases motivation. It helps counter feelings of "never doing enough" or that your efforts go unappreciated.

2. Regularly Evaluate Your Priorities

Set aside time daily to reassess your goals and priorities.
Ask yourself:
"What truly matters to me?"
"Which tasks or actions will lead to long-term success and happiness?"

This helps avoid unnecessary overload and allows you to focus on the most significant aspects of life, whether they involve work, family, or personal interests.

3. Seek Support

Sharing your concerns and challenges with colleagues, friends, or mentors can provide both emotional support and fresh perspectives. Discussions often lead to new approaches to problem-solving and a better understanding of your situation. Additionally, support from others strengthens relationships and reduces stress.

Each of these methods aims to help you not only handle challenges more effectively but also achieve greater harmony in your life.

Conclusion.

In conclusion, it's vital to remember that self-care and managing your well-being are not merely about personal comfort but form the foundation of professional success. In today's world, filled with stress and overload, maintaining a balance between work and personal life, managing emotions and stress, and regularly attending to your physical and mental health are key factors for achieving resilience and harmony.

Practicing regular self-care through relaxation techniques, setting boundaries, and carving out time for rest allows you to remain productive and successful in your career while preserving peace of mind and energy for personal accomplishments. Although this requires effort and a conscious approach, these investments in your well-being ensure long-term success and an improved quality of life.

Sustaining a healthy balance, resilience, and inner harmony is an ongoing process that, despite its challenges, delivers meaningful and valuable results for both your professional growth and personal satisfaction and happiness.

Chapter 7: Overcoming Obstacles and Challenges.

Building Resilience.

Developing resilience is a key skill for effectively handling difficulties and learning from challenging situations. It is important to understand that resilience does not mean avoiding problems or ignoring negative situations. Instead, it is the process of actively perceiving challenges as opportunities for growth, change, and self-improvement.

Seeing Opportunities in Difficult Situations.

Workplace difficulties such as project failures, negative feedback, or unexpected problems can create feelings of helplessness. However, to build resilience, it is essential to shift your perspective on these situations. Instead of viewing them as dead ends or punishments, try to see them as growth opportunities. Each challenge offers a chance to improve your skills, reconsider your approaches, or even broaden your horizons.

Example: If your project does not go as planned, rather than dwelling on the failure, analyze what went wrong and determine how these mistakes can be corrected in the future. This approach not only helps you avoid repeating the same errors but also strengthens your problem-solving capabilities.

Using Mistakes as Lessons.

A mistake is not the end but an opportunity for improvement. Each time something goes wrong, you have the chance to reevaluate your actions and refine your approach. This is a critical step toward building resilience. When you see a mistake as part of the process rather than something to fear, you begin to learn from your actions instead of avoiding failures.

Flexibility and Adaptation.

Resilience also requires flexibility. Instead of clinging to an idea or plan that isn't working, learn to adapt and seek alternative solutions. This doesn't mean giving up on your goals, but rather having the ability to adjust your course while maintaining your motivation.

Managing Stress and Emotional Overload.

Building resilience is closely tied to how you handle stress. The ability to remain calm in challenging situations and prevent negative emotions from taking control helps you maintain productivity and strengthen personal resilience. Using relaxation techniques such as meditation or breathing exercises can be an important part of this process.

Support and Self-Development.

Resilience cannot be built in isolation. Engaging with colleagues, mentors, or friends, seeking their perspectives and support, can help you see problems from a different angle. Regular self-education and skill development are also crucial for being prepared to face new challenges and difficulties.

Viewing difficulties as opportunities for growth allows you to not only enhance your personal resilience, but also significantly improve your career and personal development.

Shifting Perception.

Shifting perception is a powerful tool that enables individuals not only to navigate challenging situations, but also to use them as opportunities for personal growth. Several methods can be applied to achieve this, two of which are discussed in detail below:

1. Cognitive Reframing

Cognitive reframing involves changing how you interpret negative events. Instead of dwelling on failure, you start viewing it as an opportunity for learning and growth. This approach not only reduces stress but also transforms negativity into a resource.

Practices for Cognitive Reframing:

- Identifying Skills to Develop: When faced with a challenging situation, ask yourself: What skills can I develop from this experience? For instance, if a project fails due to poor coordination, it can serve as an opportunity to enhance teamwork and time-management skills.
- Applying Lessons to the Future: Another key question is: How can I apply this experience in the future? Mistakes provide unique opportunities to avoid repeating them. By identifying the missteps, you can sidestep these pitfalls in subsequent endeavors.
- Finding Positives in Challenges: Reflect on what positive outcomes can emerge from this challenge. Often, setbacks lead to unexpected discoveries or help uncover strengths you didn't know you had.

Example: If you experience a project failure, rather than blaming yourself or external factors, ask: What skills can I improve to prevent such errors in the future? This mindset encourages learning and highlights areas for improvement.

2. Positive Thinking.

Positive thinking does not mean ignoring problems or downplaying their significance. Instead, it is about actively choosing to focus on the positive aspects, even in the toughest situations. This approach can help reduce stress, enhance your perception of the situation, and create room for productive actions.

Examples of Positive Thinking:

- When a project fails, instead of fixating on mistakes, consider what you can take away from the experience. For instance, it might have been an excellent chance to refine your planning and risk-analysis skills.
- During stressful moments, focus on the positive elements of your work process, such as support from colleagues or your persistent efforts to find solutions. This helps build confidence, even in the face of adversity.

Positive thinking shifts your focus from problems to solutions and opportunities. While challenges won't vanish, your approach to them becomes more constructive and effective.

Research shows that individuals who practice positive thinking and cognitive reframing are more resilient in difficult situations, which fosters both professional and personal growth. These approaches improve stress management, sustain motivation, and enhance productivity.

Real-Life Examples:

Failures as Catalysts for Growth: Many successful individuals, such as John Rockefeller and Henry Ford, faced numerous failures before achieving greatness. Rockefeller went bankrupt several times, yet each failure served as a lesson that helped him rebuild stronger. His approach illustrates the importance of viewing setbacks not as endpoints but as opportunities for fresh starts.

Building Resilience: Athletes often encounter injuries and failures. For instance, Michael Jordan, who was initially cut from his high school basketball team, used this setback as motivation to work harder. Ultimately, he became one of the greatest players in history, demonstrating how challenges can fuel determination and success.

Practical Steps for Reframing Challenges.

1. Journaling: Write down your thoughts and emotions during difficult moments. This practice helps you view the situation from a different perspective and identify key takeaways or lessons.
2. Discussing with Others: Share your struggles with colleagues or mentors. A fresh perspective from someone else can often shed light on new ideas and strategies for overcoming obstacles.
3. Continuous Learning: Invest time in self-education and skill development. Each challenging situation offers lessons that can be applied in the future, so actively seek opportunities for growth.

The ability to view challenging situations as opportunities for growth are a skill that can be cultivated. Leverage your failures as stepping stones to learning and resilience. This perspective not only strengthens your ability to overcome adversity but also enhances your professional competencies. As psychologist Daniel Goleman states, "The ability to understand and manage your emotions is the key to a successful life."

Each time you face a difficulty, ask yourself: "What can I learn from this situation?" This mindset helps transform obstacles into valuable opportunities for personal and professional development.

For a deeper understanding of this topic, consider exploring resources on positive psychology and stress management, such as articles in the Positive Psychology Journal Positive Psychology Journal(https://www.apa.org) or insights from the Harvard Business Review Harvard Business Review(https://hbr.org).

Developing "Soft Power".

Soft power refers to the ability to influence others through empathy, understanding, and collaboration. Cultivating this strength allows you to effectively interact with colleagues and superiors, even in stressful situations. For example, in a conflict, instead of becoming aggressive or defensive, try to understand the other person's perspective and seek a compromise.

Developing soft power (soft skills) is critical for successful team interactions, productive collaboration, and navigating challenging situations. Below, we delve into key aspects of soft power development and practical methods to help you along the way:

1. Emotional Intelligence (EQ)

Emotional intelligence is the ability to recognize and manage your emotions while understanding and responding to the emotions of others. It's essential for effective communication, building trust, and resolving conflicts.

How to develop:

- Self-awareness: Keep a journal to record your emotional reactions to different events. This practice helps you become more aware of your feelings and their influence on your behavior.
- Active listening: Enhance your ability to truly hear and understand others. Ask questions to clarify emotions and thoughts, which benefits not only professional relationships but also personal connections.

2. Communication Skills

Effective communication involves not just clearly conveying information but also adapting your style to suit the situation and audience.

How to develop:

- Communication training: Enroll in workshops or courses on public speaking and effective communication. These improve verbal skills and boost confidence in presenting ideas.
- Feedback: Regularly seek feedback from colleagues or supervisors on your communication style. Use this input to identify and improve weaknesses.

3. Collaboration and Teamwork

Working in a team requires the ability to interact with diverse people, consider different perspectives, and align efforts toward common goals.

How to develop:

- Group projects: Participate in team initiatives or volunteer programs where you collaborate with a variety of people. These experiences enhance teamwork and delegation skills.
- Openness to others' ideas: Encourage open discussions and actively listen to colleagues' suggestions to foster a collaborative environment.

4. Conflict Resolution

Conflicts are inevitable in any team, and the ability to address them constructively is a critical component of soft power.

How to develop:

- "Win-win" approach: Strive for solutions that meet both parties' needs. For example, during a disagreement, seek compromises that preserve positive working relationships.
- Role-playing exercises: Practice resolving conflicts with colleagues or friends using various scenarios to improve your skills in handling disputes.

5. Adaptability and Flexibility

Being adaptable to change and maintaining flexibility in challenging situations is crucial for professional success.

How to develop:

- Stress resilience: Strengthen your ability to handle stress with time management techniques, breathing exercises, and other self-care practices.
- Willingness to face new challenges: Step outside your comfort zone by taking on new projects or tasks that require learning new skills.

6. Feedback and Self-Improvement

Regular feedback and a commitment to self-development are key to continuously refining your skills and achieving personal growth.

How to develop:

- Request feedback: Frequently ask colleagues and supervisors to evaluate your work and communication skills. External perspectives help you identify areas for improvement.
- Pursue self-improvement: Continuously enhance your skills by reading books, taking courses, or engaging in online training to stay updated on the latest trends and techniques.

While developing soft power takes time, the results are often worth the effort. These skills not only improve personal effectiveness but also contribute to creating a more harmonious work environment, enhancing productivity and overall job satisfaction. By cultivating empathy, understanding, and collaboration, you can navigate challenges with greater ease and build stronger relationships within your professional and personal life.

Developing a Problem-Solving Strategy.

Effective problem-solving begins with a systematic approach that prepares you for potential challenges and minimizes stress during the process. Developing a strategy involves several key steps designed to clearly understand the issue, utilize available resources, and create a reliable action plan.

Problem Identification.

Clearly defining the problem is the first and most crucial step. While it might seem obvious, we often face challenges without fully understanding their scope or exact nature. Write down the problem and answer the following key questions:

- What exactly is the issue?
- Why did it arise?
- What potential consequences could it have?

A useful tool here is the 5 Why's method, which involves repeatedly asking "Why?" to dig deeper into the root cause.

Example of the 5 Why's Method:

Problem: Your project wasn't completed on time.

1. Why wasn't the project completed on time?

Because I failed to meet the planned deadlines.

2. Why did I fail to meet the planned deadlines?

Because I underestimated the time required for some tasks.

3. Why did I underestimate the time required?

Because I didn't account for the complexity of certain tasks or create a detailed plan.

4. Why didn't I create a detailed plan?

Because I assumed I could complete everything last minute without analyzing the details.

5. Why did I assume I could complete everything last minute?

Because I relied on past experiences where I managed under pressure but didn't consider changes in the workflow.

Root Cause: Underestimating the complexity of tasks and a habit of postponing work led to a mismatch between expectations and reality.

The 5 Why's method helps uncover both immediate causes and deeper, often hidden, factors contributing to difficulties.

Resource Assessment.

Once the problem is clearly defined, evaluate the resources available to address it. These can include:

- Internal resources: Your own knowledge, experience, and skills, as well as tools and support provided by your organization.
- External resources: Network connections, colleagues, mentors, technical support, or consulting services.

For instance, if the issue involves a work process, seeking advice from a mentor or experienced colleagues might be invaluable. Assess which resources are readily accessible and which may need to be secured later.

Developing Alternatives.

Generating multiple potential solutions is critical. Explore all options, including unconventional ones, to ensure flexibility in your approach. Creating alternatives allows you to choose the best path based on the situation.

- Start with brainstorming: Write down all ideas, even those that seem impractical initially.
- Evaluate each solution considering of time, financial, and human resources required.
- Use a SWOT analysis (Strengths, Weaknesses, Opportunities, Threats) to systematically assess each option.

SWOT Analysis in Problem-Solving.

The SWOT analysis framework is a powerful tool for evaluating various solutions or situations. It helps you consider all aspects of the problem to select the most effective course of action.

1. Strengths:

Identify factors that support and enable problem resolution, such as resources, expertise, or team capabilities.

Example: If your team has expertise in a particular area, this can be a strength when implementing a solution.

2. Weaknesses:

Recognize limitations and vulnerabilities, such as time constraints, lack of resources, or gaps in knowledge.

Example: If a solution requires tools your organization doesn't have, this is a weakness.

3. Opportunities:

Explore external factors that could enhance the solution, such as trends, new technologies, or untapped resources.
Example: Partnering with an external supplier could create opportunities for better execution.

4. Threats:

Identify risks that could hinder success, including competition, regulatory changes, or unforeseen circumstances.
Example: An external threat like changing client expectations could impact the solution's success.

How to Use SWOT Analysis for Decision-Making:

1. Identify Solutions: Determine several possible solutions to the problem.
2. Evaluate Each Solution: Conduct a SWOT analysis for each solution by filling in the table of strengths, weaknesses, opportunities, and threats.
3. Comparison: After evaluating all options, compare them based on key aspects—what provides the most strengths, which threats are most critical, and what opportunities can be leveraged.
4. Decision-Making: Choose the solution that best aligns with your goals, minimizes threats, and capitalizes on opportunities.

Example of SWOT Analysis for a Project Issue:
Strengths: An experienced team, availability of resources.
Weaknesses: Limited time to complete the task.
Opportunities: Potential collaboration with a new partner.
Threats: Competitors, regulatory changes.

This analysis allows you to clearly identify which solutions are most likely to achieve the desired outcome and which might carry higher risks.

Action Plan Development.

Once you've selected the most suitable solution, it's crucial to develop a clear action plan. Break the process into sequential steps:

- Clear Planning: Define what needs to be done first, assign responsibilities, and set deadlines for each task.
- Adaptation to Changes: Be prepared to adjust the plan as new information arises, as not everything will go as expected.

Example Strategy for Responding to Criticism: If your boss expresses dissatisfaction, you can develop a plan:

- Listen Attentively: Allow the critique without interrupting.
- Ask Clarifying Questions: "Could you elaborate on the specific concerns you have?"
- Express Gratitude for Feedback: "Thank you for sharing your perspective; I will take this into consideration moving forward."
- Create an Improvement Plan: Write down specific actions you will take to address the feedback and enhance results.

This structured approach not only works in professional settings but can also improve personal interactions by fostering constructive responses to criticism.

Key Takeaways:

Developing a problem-solving strategy is valuable not only for professional scenarios, but also for personal situations.

Clear problem identification, effective resource utilization, generation of alternatives, and action planning form the foundation for successfully overcoming challenges. A systematic approach ensures better outcomes, reduces stress, and builds confidence in tackling future difficulties.

Real-Life Examples:

Let's consider an example where an employee faces criticism from their boss. Instead of perceiving the criticism as a personal attack, they can use it to evaluate their work and identify areas for improvement. This requires not only resilience, but also active listening skills and openness to feedback.

Problem-Solving Tips:

- Practice Self-Reflection: Regularly allocate time to evaluate your reactions to challenging situations. This helps you understand the emotions you experience and how they influence your behavior.
- Discuss Issues with Colleagues: A fresh perspective can often provide new ideas and approaches to problem-solving.
- Be Open to Change: Flexibility in your methods and readiness to adapt to new conditions will help you manage unexpected challenges effectively.
- Take Care of Your Mental Health: Stress and difficulties can take a toll on your well-being. Make time for rest and recovery to maintain high productivity levels.

By building resilience and developing a problem-solving strategy, you can handle workplace challenges more effectively while fostering stronger and more productive relationships with your colleagues and supervisors.

Chapter 8: Turning Conflict into Collaboration

Conflict with a boss or colleagues can seem like an insurmountable obstacle, especially when the other party appears difficult or stubborn. However, conflict doesn't have to be a deadlock—it can become a springboard for growth and improved interaction. Historical examples, negotiation theories, and scientific research demonstrate that well-managed conflict strengthens relationships and fosters teamwork. This chapter explores how to transform conflict into collaboration using techniques that promote mutual respect, creativity, and the achievement of shared goals.

Understanding the Nature of Conflict.

Conflict arises when two or more parties perceive that their goals, interests, values, or resources are in opposition. In the workplace, this may manifest as differing opinions on priorities, resource allocation, or task execution. Conflict is not inherently negative; if managed correctly, it can drive innovation, improve workflows, and even strengthen team spirit. However, if left unchecked, conflict can lead to dissatisfaction, mistrust, and reduced productivity.

The Scientific Perspective on Conflict.

Research by De Dreu and Gelfand (2008) highlights that well-resolved conflicts can foster creativity. They found that conflicts leading to constructive discussions and the enrichment of perspectives often result in innovative solutions, more efficient approaches, and improved methods. The key is not to eliminate conflict entirely but to leverage it as a catalyst for professional growth and better outcomes. This principle applies to workplace teams and broader organizational disputes, where engaging diverse viewpoints leads to optimal solutions.

Historical Example: Roosevelt and Churchill.

A compelling historical example of productive conflict resolution is the relationship between U.S. President Franklin D. Roosevelt and British Prime Minister Winston Churchill during World War II. Despite ongoing disagreements about strategy—Roosevelt prioritized defeating Nazi Germany through a second front in Europe, while Churchill advocated for strengthening operations in the Mediterranean—their ability to compromise forged a powerful allied coalition. Their collaborative efforts not only played a pivotal role in winning the war but also laid the groundwork for postwar alliances that shaped global order. Roosevelt and Churchill demonstrated that even amidst tension, productive collaboration can lead to personal and collective success.

Successful conflict resolution is more than just resolving immediate disagreements; it is an opportunity to improve processes, develop skills, and establish long-term partnerships. Whether in corporate settings or international relations, leveraging conflict for positive outcomes can enhance relationships and drive collective success.

Using Negotiation Techniques.

Transforming conflict into collaboration often hinges on effective negotiation techniques. Below are actionable strategies to foster constructive dialogue and resolve disputes while building stronger relationships.

1. Active Listening

Active listening forms the cornerstone of successful negotiations and interactions. It involves focusing not just on what the other person says but also on their emotions and intentions. This approach helps uncover the underlying needs and motivations of the opposing party, leading to more productive outcomes.

How It Works: Active listening includes paraphrasing the speaker's words to confirm understanding and build trust.

Example: If someone criticizes your work, instead of becoming defensive, you might say:

"I understand that you're concerned about a specific issue. Could you elaborate on what you find most challenging?"

This shifts the interaction from defensiveness to constructive dialogue.

2. Finding Common Ground.

Focusing on shared interests rather than differences is essential during negotiations. When parties concentrate on mutual goals, it creates opportunities for win-win solutions.

How It Works: Instead of dwelling on demands, dig deeper to uncover the motivations behind them.

Example: If a teammate emphasizes a tight deadline, ask, "What outcomes are most critical for you in this project?"

This opens the door to finding a solution that satisfies both parties' interests.

Scientific Backing: Fisher, Ury, and Patton's 2011 research emphasizes prioritizing interests over positions. Understanding the underlying needs leads to more flexible and effective solutions.

3. Using Neutral Language

The language you use during negotiations can either escalate tension or pave the way for resolution. Avoiding blame and emotional outbursts is crucial.

How It Works: Neutral phrasing focuses on facts and solutions rather than assigning blame.

Example: Instead of saying,

"You're always late for meetings," reframe it as,

"I've noticed some delays in starting meetings on time. Is there something we can adjust to help improve this?"

This approach fosters collaboration rather than defensiveness.

4. Reframing Conflict as a Shared Task

Viewing conflict as a mutual challenge rather than a confrontation encourages collaborative problem-solving.

How It Works: Shift your mindset from "me vs. you" to "us vs. the problem."

Example: If faced with an unrealistic deadline, say,

"I understand the importance of meeting this timeline. Let's discuss how we can make the project feasible while maintaining quality."

This approach invites the other party to work with you rather than against you.

5. Using Mediation for Conflict Resolution

Mediation is a valuable tool when negotiations reach an impasse. A neutral third party can balance perspectives and guide discussions toward a constructive resolution.

How It Works: Mediators structure the dialogue and propose solutions that satisfy both sides.

Example: The 1978 Camp David Accords demonstrated the power of mediation, where U.S. President Jimmy Carter facilitated a historic agreement between Egypt and Israel by fostering compromise and mutual understanding.

6. Constructive Feedback and De-escalation

Constructive feedback minimizes misunderstandings and reduces tension. Using "I-statements" can express concerns without assigning blame.

How It Works: Focus on your feelings and needs instead of accusing the other person.

Example: Rather than saying, "You always change deadlines at the last minute,"

reframe it as,

"I feel overwhelmed when deadlines shift unexpectedly. Can we discuss how to manage this better in the future?"

Scientific Backing: Gottman and Silver's 1999 study highlights the importance of maintaining a 5:1 ratio of positive to negative interactions for successful conflict resolution.

7. Learning from Conflict

Post-conflict analysis is crucial for improving communication and negotiation skills. Reflecting on what worked and what didn't allows you to handle future disputes more effectively.
How It Works: Reviewing conflicts helps identify successful strategies and areas for improvement.
Example: After a tense discussion with a colleague, evaluate what approaches led to constructive outcomes and brainstorm alternative strategies for unresolved issues.
Real-Life Example: Oprah Winfrey exemplified exceptional negotiation skills during her interview with Prince Harry and Meghan Markle. By balancing the interests of all parties, she conducted a successful interview while maintaining editorial independence.

Building a Common Goal.

The Importance of Establishing a Common Goal.
A common goal is a foundational element of successful teamwork. It unites team members around a shared direction, strengthens mutual trust, and sustains motivation throughout a project. Without a clearly defined common goal, teams can lose focus, leading to confusion, conflicts, disengagement, and reduced productivity.

1. Unifying the Team:

When all team members share a common goal, it enables seamless and effective collaboration. This minimizes situational disagreements by prioritizing the project's success over individual preferences. Research shows that common goals enhance both performance and engagement as employees feel part of something greater (Hackman, 2009).

2. Increasing Motivation:

Seeing how their efforts contribute to a collective objective boosts individual motivation. Team members understand their work's impact, making their tasks more meaningful. A clearly defined common goal clarifies how individual contributions fit into the larger success of the project, particularly important in multitasking environments (Edmondson, 2012).

3. Reducing Uncertainty:

A shared goal serves as an anchor for all participants, which is particularly critical in complex or uncertain situations. Understanding that everyone is working towards the same outcome alleviates stress and ambiguity. Studies confirm that a clear goal helps teams adapt more quickly to changes while maintaining high levels of efficiency (Morgeson, et al., 2010).

4. Fostering a Collaborative Culture:

Defining a common goal cultivates an open and inclusive atmosphere. When all team members recognize their opinions and efforts as valuable, it strengthens relationships, lowers barriers, and encourages the exchange of ideas. It is essential to ensure everyone feels heard and valued, which promotes better team dynamics (Katzenbach & Smith, 1993).

By building a shared goal, teams can boost productivity, motivation, and collaboration while creating a positive environment conducive to success.

1. Defining the Common Goal.

Establishing a clear and unified goal is the first and most critical step in fostering successful collaboration within any team or project. When all participants align their efforts toward a shared outcome, it significantly enhances understanding and minimizes conflicts.

How It Works:

Defining a common goal helps the team focus on results rather than differences. For instance, when developing a new product, emphasizing the goal of delivering a quality and user-friendly product can unite the team despite differing approaches and working styles.

Example:

During a meeting, you might say: "Our goal is to create a product that's both convenient and valuable for our users. While we may have different viewpoints, it's crucial to remember that our project's success relies on teamwork."

2. Engaging All Stakeholders

Actively involving all participants in discussions and decision-making fosters an atmosphere of openness and trust. This enhances commitment to the common goal and ensures diverse perspectives are considered, leading to better outcomes.

How It Works:

Providing everyone with the opportunity to voice their ideas and opinions fosters a sense of ownership and strengthens team cohesion. This inclusive approach helps identify potential weaknesses in a plan or solution that might otherwise go unnoticed.

Example:

During team meetings, ask open-ended questions to encourage discussion, such as:

"How do you view this solution?" or "What suggestions do you have to improve this process?"

This approach gives each team member the chance to contribute and feel valued in achieving the common goal.

3. Creating an Action Plan

Once the common goal is defined and all participants are engaged, the next step is to develop a detailed action plan. This involves dividing tasks, assigning responsibilities, and setting specific deadlines for each phase.

How It Works:

A well-structured and detailed plan of action eliminates confusion and ensures everyone understands their responsibilities and deadlines. It ensures all efforts are directed toward the shared goal.

Example:

Assign specific tasks to each team member with deadlines and intermediate checkpoints. For instance:

"Anna, you'll work on developing the prototype by the end of the month, and Ivan, you'll handle testing. Afterward, we'll meet to discuss the results."

This approach helps track progress and adjust actions as needed, increasing the likelihood of achieving the goal.

This also allows for tracking progress and adjusting actions as needed, which increases the likelihood of successfully achieving the goal.

Together, these steps help create a structure in which the team works cohesively, contributing to overall success.

Examples:

Successful Conflict Resolution Example:

A company faced a conflict between its marketing and sales departments over how to promote a new product. Both teams were at odds and unable to find common ground. The manager organized a meeting where both teams could express their concerns. By employing active listening techniques, the manager identified their shared goal: maximizing sales for the new product. This alignment allowed the teams to collaborate on a unified strategy, ultimately leading to increased company revenue.

Example of Failure:

In another case, a company failed to involve all stakeholders in its decision-making process. Leadership made unilateral decisions without consulting employees, which led to dissatisfaction and conflicts. Employees felt ignored and undervalued, causing a decline in motivation and productivity. This lack of inclusiveness escalated tensions and hindered overall company performance.

Tips for Problem-Solving.

1. Approach Conflicts Constructively

Conflicts are inevitable in any workplace or personal environment. However, the key is to approach them constructively to prevent escalation or negative consequences. Before engaging in discussions, try to objectively assess the situation. Identify the root cause of the conflict and consider solutions that can help both parties reach a compromise. This requires mindfulness, emotional detachment, and a focus on problem-solving rather than assigning blame.

Scientific Insight:
A constructive approach to conflict resolution has been shown to improve mental health and workplace relationships. For example, a study by Benjamin B. Blackwell and colleagues (2012) found that constructive conflict resolution techniques significantly reduce stress levels and enhance team productivity.

2. Address Emotional Aspects

Emotions play a crucial role in conflict situations. When individuals feel their emotions are ignored or dismissed, conflicts can intensify. Openly discussing emotional aspects helps reduce tension and fosters mutual understanding. Empathy and attention to the emotional state of the other party create an environment for honest and open communication, paving the way for effective solutions.

Implementation Tips:
Use active listening and express your emotions through "I-statements" (e.g., "I feel frustrated when I don't receive feedback"). This minimizes defensiveness and fosters an atmosphere of mutual respect and understanding, particularly in emotionally charged situations.

3. Stay Open to Change

Flexibility and a willingness to adapt your position are essential for resolving conflicts. This does not mean conceding on every point, but being open to re-evaluating your approaches and perspectives can be critical. When conflicts remain unresolved due to stubbornness, adaptability can help break the impasse and pave the way for compromise.

Scientific Backing:
Research in conflict resolution demonstrates that flexibility and adaptability foster better collaboration and stronger long-term relationships (De Dreu, 2010). It also contributes to a healthier workplace atmosphere and improved productivity.

These approaches not only enable effective conflict resolution but also help develop communication and understanding skills that are valuable in any situation.

Brief Conclusion:
Conflicts are unavoidable, but they do not have to lead to discord or inefficiency. By applying active listening techniques, identifying shared goals, and utilizing mediation, disagreements can become opportunities for collaboration. Historical and real-life examples demonstrate that well-managed conflicts can enhance creativity and strengthen relationships.

Every conflict is an opportunity for growth. Approach it with curiosity and patience, aiming to find common ground. Developing conflict resolution skills not only improves relationships with colleagues and supervisors but also supports your professional growth.

Transforming conflict into collaboration requires effort, understanding, and a willingness to engage in dialogue. By leveraging active listening, seeking shared goals, and fostering an atmosphere of openness, each conflict can become a chance to build stronger connections and improve outcomes.

Conclusion: The Art of Harmony in the Workplace

Building harmonious relationships at work is a challenging yet achievable process that requires patience, flexibility, and a willingness to change. Effective interaction with a supervisor—especially one perceived as difficult or incompetent—depends not only on professional skills but also on the ability to manage your emotions and behavior.

Adaptability as a Key Skill.

In a rapidly changing world with increasing demands for professionalism, adaptability has become a critical skill for success. It is not just about adjusting to external circumstances, but also about viewing challenges as opportunities for growth. Adaptability requires flexibility, a willingness to try new approaches, continuous learning, and the resilience to handle setbacks without losing motivation.

When your supervisor assigns challenging tasks or sets high expectations, see these as opportunities for self-improvement. Instead of viewing these demands as excessive or unreasonable, look for the chance to learn something new, enhance your skills, and step beyond your comfort zone. This perspective not only strengthens your professional reputation but also builds a more resilient career in the long term.

How to Adapt: Practical Tips.

- Understand the Context of Change: Before embracing change, take time to understand why it is happening. For example, if the organization is shifting its strategic focus—such as transitioning to new technologies or restructuring teams—understand the reasons and how they impact your workflow.
- Courage in Learning New Skills: Fear of change often stems from the need to acquire new skills. However, the courage to learn and apply new tools and approaches not only helps alleviate stress but also makes you a more valuable employee.
- Embrace Challenges as Growth Opportunities: Avoid perceiving challenges as threats or stressors. Instead, see them as chances to upgrade your expertise, expand your abilities, and boost your self-esteem.

The Practice of Self-Reflection

Regular self-reflection is crucial for improving adaptability. Keeping a self-reflection journal helps track your progress and analyze how you handle difficult situations. By documenting your experiences, reactions, and lessons learned, you can identify which strategies work best and which areas need improvement.

Example: After completing a challenging project, write about how you reacted to difficulties, what helped resolve issues, and what caused unnecessary stress. This process will help you approach future tasks with greater awareness and discover new ways to handle challenges effectively.

Applying Techniques in Practice

To build confidence, it is important not only to understand theories, but also to actively apply them in real-life situations. Techniques like active listening, negotiation, conflict management, and feedback require regular practice to become natural and effective in daily work.

Example of Active Listening:

If criticized by your supervisor, avoid becoming defensive or emotionally reactive. Instead, use active listening:

"I understand that you're concerned about the quality of the report. What changes do you think would improve the outcome?"

This approach reduces tension, demonstrates maturity, and shows a willingness to learn and improve.

Benefits of This Approach.

- Stress Reduction: Criticism is no longer perceived as a personal attack but as a helpful tool for growth.
- Building Trust: Such behavior strengthens relationships with colleagues and supervisors by showing openness to feedback and collaboration.

Adaptability, active use of various work methods, and regular self-reflection are key elements for not only overcoming challenges but also for personal and professional growth.

In today's fast-paced world, where change is constant, the ability to adapt and enhance your skills is the foundation of a successful career and personal development. By embracing challenges, reflecting on your experiences, and actively applying effective strategies, you can turn obstacles into opportunities and achieve greater harmony and fulfillment in the workplace.

Self-Management as the Ultimate Mastery.

Self-management is the ability to control one's emotions, behavior, and reactions in various situations. In the workplace, where stress, pressure, and ambiguity often converge, maintaining inner harmony and making well-reasoned decisions becomes not only a useful skill but also the foundation for personal and professional growth. It is important to recognize that while we cannot control the behavior of others—be it managers or colleagues—we can influence how we respond to their actions. This requires self-awareness, discipline, and the application of specific strategies.

1. Emotional Control

Emotions are natural reactions to external events. However, when they overly influence decision-making or interactions with others, they can create problems. The ability to control emotions does not mean suppressing them but managing them effectively. For instance, recognizing your emotions in moments of stress or irritation and allowing yourself time to reflect can prevent impulsive decisions that might harm relationships or lead to undesirable outcomes.

2. Mindfulness and Self-Reflection

One of the most powerful tools for self-management is mindfulness. It is the ability to be present in the moment, observe your thoughts and reactions, and avoid succumbing to automatic emotional responses. Self-reflection is also crucial for understanding how your behavior and decisions impact the workplace atmosphere and relationships. Regularly reflecting on your actions helps identify weaknesses and work on improving them.

3. Making Reasoned Decisions.

Mastery of self-management also includes the ability to make decisions based on reason rather than emotions. When faced with a challenging situation, it is important to pause and weigh all potential consequences. This involves:

- Gathering and analyzing information before making a decision.
- Evaluating all alternatives and risks.
- Making decisions with consideration of long-term goals rather than immediate emotions.

4. Maintaining Calm in Stressful Situations.

When faced with a problem or unexpected challenge, maintaining calm is a demonstration of inner strength. This does not mean ignoring stress, but rather managing its impact. One technique for this is breathing exercises, which help restore balance to the nervous system and enable you to act without succumbing to panic.

5. Overcoming Stereotypes and Automatic Responses.

Many of us often act out of habit, including in response to stress or conflicts, automatically choosing certain reactions even when they are not always optimal. To manage oneself effectively, it is important to identify these habits and patterns, make conscious decisions, and adjust behavior when necessary.

Self-management is the foundation for effective interaction and successful work. These skills can be developed through mindfulness, self-reflection, emotional control, and thoughtful decision-making. Given that stressful situations are inevitable in a professional environment, cultivating these qualities is essential for sustaining both personal and professional growth.

Viewing Difficult Experiences as Opportunities for Growth.

Challenges and disagreements are an inevitable part of working life. While many aim to avoid conflicts or difficult situations, it is crucial to recognize that these moments can be the catalyst for personal and professional growth. Instead of perceiving hardships as negative or destructive, consider them opportunities for evolution and self-improvement.

Why Challenges Are Essential for Growth

1. Developing Emotional Resilience:

Overcoming workplace challenges strengthens inner resilience. Facing difficulties teaches individuals not only to solve problems, but also to manage emotions during stressful situations. This leads to better control over moods and reactions, a valuable skill in professional life.

For example, criticism can sting, but it provides a chance to improve. Instead of becoming defensive, consider how you can use feedback to enhance your performance.

2. Enhancing Problem-Solving Skills

Difficult situations demand decision-making, information analysis, and exploring alternatives. These processes train the ability to make well-founded and effective decisions, essential for developing leadership and analytical qualities. For example, resolving conflicts with colleagues or completing tasks under uncertainty fosters mental flexibility and decision-making skills under pressure.

3. Learning from Mistakes

Mistakes are not a cause for despair but an opportunity for growth. Analyzing the reasons behind failures and contemplating alternative approaches helps avoid repeating the same errors and accelerates skill development. Mistakes provide valuable feedback that can guide improvement. For example, if a project fails, take time to identify where the breakdown occurred, what decisions led to the outcome, and how to adjust your approach moving forward.

4. Building Confidence

Each successful experience of overcoming difficulties boosts self-confidence. When a person realizes they can handle challenges, their self-esteem grows stronger. This process enhances the ability to tackle even greater difficulties in the future.

Confidence emerges when we understand that we can endure even the most unpleasant situations and learn valuable lessons from them.

Workplace challenges and conflicts are not the end but the beginning of a new phase of personal and professional growth. By overcoming them, you not only develop your technical skills but also essential qualities such as emotional maturity, flexibility, and self-regulation. In the long term, this strengthens your confidence and empowers you to reach new heights.

Harmonious Workplace Relationships: A Path to Professional Mastery.

In the workplace, relationships between colleagues, superiors, and subordinates play a critical role in achieving success and personal satisfaction. Harmony within a team and the ability to work effectively with others are not just byproducts of a positive atmosphere—they are essential for productivity. In professional life, it is crucial to find a balance between personal goals and collective interests, between striving for results and maintaining healthy interpersonal relationships.

What Are Harmonious Workplace Relationships?

Harmonious workplace relationships occur when people within a team can effectively work together despite differences in personal preferences, perspectives, and working styles. This doesn't imply an absence of conflicts or disagreements, but rather the ability to resolve them constructively and move toward shared goals.

1. Emotional Intelligence: The ability to understand and manage your emotions, as well as recognize the emotions of others, forms the foundation of strong workplace relationships. Emotional intelligence helps navigate challenging situations, resolve disagreements, and fosters effective collaboration. For example, demonstrating empathy toward colleagues builds trust, which in turn enhances teamwork.
2. Openness and Communication: Transparency and honesty are the cornerstones of trust. When individuals openly share their thoughts, concerns, and ideas, it leads to better understanding and more efficient collaboration. Open communication prevents misunderstandings and facilitates early problem resolution.
3. Collaboration and Mutual Support: In a healthy workplace, colleagues support one another, work as a team, and avoid unnecessary competition. This means individuals are willing to share knowledge, assist with tasks, and collectively work toward common goals.

How to Foster Harmony in Workplace Relationships?

1. Self-Management: Building healthy relationships with others begins with managing your own emotions and behavior. This includes staying calm in stressful situations, avoiding impulsive decisions, and controlling reactions to external irritants. When you can manage yourself, collaborating with others becomes much easier.
2. Understanding Others' Needs: Recognizing what matters to your colleagues helps tailor your behavior and approaches. For instance, some people may prefer detailed information and clear instructions, while others may thrive with creative freedom and autonomy. The ability to adapt to individual needs fosters an atmosphere of respect and trust.
3. Balancing Personal Goals and Collective Interests: It's essential to remember that a successful career depends not only on personal efforts but also on the ability to contribute to a shared objective. Harmony is achieved when personal ambitions align with the interests of the team or company. Balancing personal aspirations with collective goals helps maintain positive relationships in the long term.

Why Is It Important to Maintain Harmonious Relationships?

1. Boosting Productivity: When colleagues work in an environment of mutual respect and understanding, their productivity increases significantly. Open communication and collaboration lead to quicker decision-making and improved work quality.
2. Improving Workplace Morale: Positive workplace relationships foster an atmosphere where people feel comfortable and motivated. This reduces stress levels, enhances employees' mental and emotional well-being, and contributes to overall satisfaction.
3. Personal Growth and Career Advancement: The ability to build harmonious relationships with colleagues supports career progression. Those who can collaborate effectively and resolve conflicts constructively often emerge as strong leaders and gain more opportunities for advancement.

Harmonious workplace relationships are more than just a product of good manners—they are a strategic foundation for career success. The ability to work with people, maintain healthy relationships, and build trust within a team are skills that can be developed. It's essential to remember that workplace harmony starts with you: managing yourself and prioritizing your emotional well-being is key to fostering successful and enduring connections with colleagues.

Remember, successful relationships with supervisors and colleagues require not only professional expertise but also emotional flexibility, patience, and a genuine willingness to collaborate. Don't fear challenges—they are the opportunities that help you grow and unlock your potential. The more you practice self-management and interpersonal skills, the more confident you will feel in any situation.

If, after reading this book and applying the described practices, you are still convinced that your boss is incompetent, then I recommend taking the following steps for professional development and reading the book "My Boss Is Stupid! Mastering the Art of Managing True Incompetence".

Bibliography:

Barrios, R. (2016). Active listening: Enhancing understanding and building rapport. Journal of Communication Studies, 24(3), 45-58.

Cohen, S., & Janicki-Deverts, D. (2012). Who's stressed? Distributions of psychological stress in the United States in probability samples from 1983, 2006, and 2009. Journal of Applied Social Psychology, 42(6), 1320-1334.

De Dreu, C. K. W., & Gelfand, M. J. (2008). Conflict resolution and creativity: Leveraging diversity for optimal solutions. American Psychologist, 63(6), 609-622.

Dirks, K. T., & Ferrin, D. L. (2002). Trust in leadership: Meta-analytic findings and implications for research and practice. Journal of Applied Psychology, 87(4), 611-628.

Pease, A., & Pease, B. (2017). The definitive book of body language: The hidden meaning behind people's gestures and expressions. Bantam.

Rebar, A. L., Stanton, R., Geard, D., Short, C., Duncan, M. J., & Vandelanotte, C. (2015). A meta-meta-analysis of the effect of physical activity on depression and anxiety in non-clinical adult populations. Health Psychology Review, 9(3), 366-378.

Riggs, S. (2019). Seeking feedback: Enhancing workplace communication. International Journal of Business Communication, 56(2), 278-295.

Werner, P., Norton, M. I., & Ariely, D. (2018). Clear and concise communication: Reducing misunderstandings. Harvard Business Review, 96(2), 123-129

Printed in Great Britain
by Amazon